# Volkswagen
# Transporter

First published in March 2008

A catalogue record for this book is available from the British Library

ISBN 978 1 84425 406 4

Library of Congress control no. 2007940705

Design and layout by Richard Parsons

All photographs from the author's collection except:
Ken Cservenka (24, 28, 42, 53, 58 top, 60top, 88, 90, 94btm, 114btm, 115top)
O'Connors Campers (169btm)

Published by Haynes Publishing, Sparkford, Yeovil, Somerset BA22 7JJ, UK.
Tel: 01963 442030 Fax: 01963 440001
Int. tel: +44 1963 442030
Int. fax: +44 1963 440001
E-mail: sales@haynes.co.uk
Website: www.haynes.co.uk

Haynes North America Inc., 861 Lawrence Drive, Newbury Park, California 91320, USA

Printed and bound in Britain by J. H. Haynes & Co. Ltd,
Sparkford, Yeovil, Somerset BA22 7JJ

## ACKNOWLEDGEMENTS

Various people in the ever-growing band of Transporter enthusiasts deserve my unending thanks for the help they have given me in bringing this project to a successful conclusion.

Fellow authors Malcolm Bobbitt, Richard Copping and Ken Cservenka all provided invaluable information essential to the compilation of this book, as did David Eccles, editor of *Volkswagen Camper and Commercial* magazine and author of several volumes covering various aspects of Transporter development and life. Also grateful thanks to Ken Cservenka who provided a number of images for me to use when my own photo library proved inadequate. Meetings in the past with Laurence Meredith, who wrote about the Transporter when interest in it was wholly subservient to the euphoria surrounding the Beetle, probably sparked my initial interest in contemplating a volume dedicated to what is now the most popular old Volkswagen of all. Well-known long-term Volkswagen enthusiast Brian Screaton shared some valuable archive material that has undoubtedly added to the overall content of this book.

A number of enthusiastic owners went out of their way not only to allow me to photograph their vehicles but also to accede to my demands for the Transporter in question to be turned at various intervals, after first travelling to an appropriate location. Particular thanks in this field go to Robert Brunch, Mark Buckingham, Richard Burrows, Stuart and Doreen Burrows, Nigel Collier, Tim Crone, Guy Eastment, Fraser Easton, Huw Frances, Matt Lancaster, Alan Meldrum, Adele Newman, Paul Olma, Adrian Pilkington, Russell Ritchie, Brian Robertson, Catriona Ross, Scott Sherry, Bob Stirzaker, Ian Tait, Alan Ward and Fritz Yarwood.

A special word of thanks must go to a nucleus of members of the Split Screen Van Club, all of whose friendship is highly valued. Likewise, to the organisers of some of the many shows dedicated to, or at least featuring, Transporters, who allowed me to disrupt their proceedings or on occasion afforded special entry to an event, a big thank you.

I am particularly indebted to Richard Hulin of Richard Hulin Motor Engineers, Gloucester for his invaluable help with the issues surrounding non-standard engine transplants and other technical matters. Valuable help was offered by O'Connors Campers, Dormobile and Paris Beetles in respect of information relating to both elevating and sun roofs.

Finally, a big thank you to my family for their understanding during the days and evenings I have been busy writing this book, and for their patience while I diverted to photograph yet another Transporter.

Jonathan Harvey, 2007

Haynes Enthusiast Guide

# Volkswagen
# Transporter

Jonathan Harvey

# VOLKSWAGEN TRANSPORTER
# CONTENTS

# INTRODUCTION
# THE TRANSPORTER PHENOMENON

Incredible as it might sound, well in excess of 25,000 people attended a single show dedicated solely to the VW Transporter recently. Every nook and cranny of the once over ample showground involved was wedged full of Transporters; ranging from the sparklingly pristine, often better than new Concours examples, decidedly well-worn and lived-in daily drivers, patched and rusty buckets awaiting much more than cosmetic surgery, customised queens each a whirlwind of phantasmagoria, to homely and petted Campers in their droves, each and every one of them loved dearly by their owners.

The Transporter phenomenon has been gathering pace for a good time now, forcing ever-upwards asking prices and not only those of the smiley-faced first-generation, or 'Splitty' (split-windscreen), models that have unquestionably reached genuine classic ranking. The second-mortgage significance of this model and, for today's usage, its semi-impractical status, first increased the prospects of its panoramically attractive successor, nicknamed the 'Bay' (bay window). When this still visually up-to-date model had likewise spiralled to values out of step with, for example, economy camping, slowly but surely, the once unloved third-generation Transporter began to be absorbed into the enthusiasts' world, even being endowed with its own nickname of the 'Wedge'. Carefully cultivated affection once more played its hand and prices here too have crept silently, but steadily, upwards.

An apparently unending wave of nostalgia for the designs and inherent quality of products of a bygone age has undoubtedly been a contributory factor in the ongoing Transporter success story. Likewise, the extraordinary growth in the last ten years of making full use of every available leisure-time moment in the great outdoors has been of equal importance to the vehicle. With the Transporter and only with the Transporter, at least in its numerous camper guises, is it possible to indulge one with the other and

therein undoubtedly lies the heart of the matter. No Beetle can do this, nor can a pretty Karmann Ghia; this is the Transporter phenomenon! Two more factors play an important part here. First, there's the ready availability of rust-free Bays and Wedges from the sun-soaked parts of the world to consider. Not cheap admittedly, but on hand to drive away at a price that will be less than that of the average modern saloon, full of nostalgia, and not a king's ransom to insure or to keep in tip-top mechanical condition. Second, a camper is one of the few vehicles that can be legitimately updated, altered, or amended without any risk of being accused of destroying its originality. A camper is a home on wheels – to do with as you wish!

What this book aims to do is draw together all aspects of the Transporter story in a single volume, something that hasn't been successfully achieved previously. The intention is to summarise the first 40 years of the Transporter's history, a fascinating exercise in itself, while also getting down to the nuts and bolts of what makes it tick and how an owner can keep it purring. The plentiful variations developed by Volkswagen are described, as are the camping conversions devised by companies here in Britain, in the USA and, of course, in Germany. Crucial guidelines for anyone contemplating a purchase, be it a first or a fiftieth, are covered, while customising the body and beefing up the performance, both essential elements of ownership to more than a few, are explored.

Thanks to its encyclopaedic nature, some will see this book as indulging the knowledgeable enthusiast with more than just mere revision, while others will regard it as invaluable to those delving into the Transporter business for the first time. What is indisputable is that the old Volkswagen of the moment, and a very long moment it appears set to be, fully deserves its following and equally warrants its description as a phenomenon of 21st century motoring.

# CHAPTER I
# A TRANSPORTER HISTORY LESSON

Untainted by Nazism, the birth of the Transporter came as the dark shadow of recent war finally receded. Volkswagen's commercial vehicle was the brainchild of an entrepreneurial Dutchman made reality by the combination of a factory with the necessary spare capacity to produce it, and the foresight of a former Opel director who by this time was in charge at Wolfsburg.

## A home for the KdF-Wagen

In January 1938, land had been summarily requisitioned by the Nazi government to build a factory suitable for the production of their people's car. To us this was the Volkswagen, or unofficially the Beetle; to them (or at least with effect from the foundation-stone laying ceremony) it became the Kraft-durch-Freude Wagen, or Strength-through-Joy Car. Highly ambitious, but equally fanciful, plans amounting to the production of as many as 10,000-cars on a monthly basis by December 1939, demanded that the factory we know today as Wolfsburg was built on a scale sufficient to cope with such volume. This was duly achieved before war broke out, with the plant boasting an initial frontage of 1,350 metres, (1,476 yards).

Ferdinand Porsche, the people's car creator, planned to build and develop a number of variations on the saloon's body and chassis, but the relentless advance of Hitler's war brought his progress to a grinding halt. Porsche was swiftly diverted in the direction of the Reich's military needs and, amongst other projects, versions of the KdF-Wagen that included first and foremost the revolutionary all-terrain Kübelwagen, and the equally remarkable multi-tasking Schwimmwagen. As the war progressed and availability of both fuel and materials evaporated, Porsche had to improvise, even producing wood-burning vehicles that bore a physical resemblance to the people's car, but

utilised the Kübel's running gear. As a consequence of hostilities, the closest Porsche came to designing a commercial vehicle was the unquestionably bizarre-looking design which saw the KdF-Wagen's rear side and back windows, plus the appropriate roof section, removed and replaced by little more than a garden shed unceremoniously dumped on the car's truncated body.

## Survival leading to security

With the fabric of the factory 60 per cent bomb damaged, the former KdF-Wagen plant fell into the British Zone of control after the war. Porsche had fled the country and key Nazi workers and sympathisers had similarly vanished when they knew their cause to be lost. A British REME officer, Major Ivan Hirst, was duly despatched to take control and, against the odds, Beetle production resumed. As there was no long-term intention to retain control of either the factory or its output, it was inevitable that a German management team would one day take over the officially ownerless factory's running. On 1 January 1948, an ex-Opel director, Heinz Nordhoff, took on the mantle of director-general. Principal amongst his aims was to 'make ... [Wolfsburg] into the greatest car factory in Europe'. An experienced manufacturer with a burning ambition to succeed not only for himself but also for the greater good of Germany, Nordhoff must have questioned whether the point would ever be reached when the Nazi fantasy factory might be utilised to full capacity.

## The *Plattenwagen* sows a seed

Although perfecting the car, which Nordhoff deemed initially to have 'more flaws than a dog has fleas', was his first priority, it is realistic to assume that an idea presented to him for commercial vehicle production

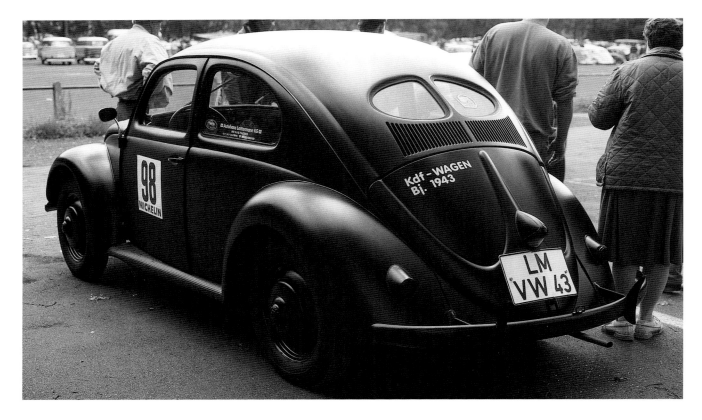

met favour in part due to capacity issues. The
proposal came from Dutchman, Ben Pon, the first
man to import the Beetle, who had been present
at the factory sufficiently often to witness flatbed
trucks at work carrying goods from one area to

another. Created by Ivan Hirst as a direct result of
the withdrawal of army transport, the Plattenwagen
utilised the chassis of the Kübelwagen and Beetle
running gear. The vehicle featured a box-like cab that
was placed directly over the rear-mounted engine.

Aware of the potential merits of this strange
contraption, Pon endeavoured to convince the
necessary powers in Holland of the vehicle's
merit for import. However, this was not to be, as
the Dutch transport authority condemned the
Plattenwagen as inappropriate, thanks to the driving
position being at the rear rather than the front
of the vehicle. Although temporarily thwarted,
it wasn't long before Pon bounced back with his
now legendary sketch of a box-like van, a crude
but inspirational forerunner of the first-generation
Transporter. Ivan Hirst was duly impressed with
what he saw; a vehicle designed to carry 750kg
(1,654lb), with its engine at the rear and a driving
position over the steering at the front. Sadly, Hirst
and Pon failed to convince Charles Radclyffe,
the man charged with overall responsibility for
engineering construction in the British Zone.
His concern was that the factory was already
overstretched, as at the time each Beetle produced
took over 300 man-hours to produce.

## Gathering pace towards Transporter production

A little over 12 months later in the autumn of 1948, and with Nordhoff firmly in the driving seat, the situation was very different. Pon's plan was presented again and the factory's technical director, Alfred Haesner, was charged with producing prototypes as soon as possible. His brief was to ignore practices of the past and to use Pon's sketch as the basis for a truly revolutionary proposal. On 20 November Nordhoff was duly presented with two designs – one with a flat-faced cab and the other offering a raked front. The director general chose the latter and in order that costs could be kept to a minimum, as many Beetle parts as possible were incorporated into the design. Sadly, utilisation of the saloon's albeit extended chassis proved to be its downfall. Testing of the first prototype, which had begun on 9 March 1949, ground to a halt after just three weeks, as the chassis twisted and buckled under the weight of materials placed in the load section. Fortunately, all was not lost, as the original design was tweaked into

← Utilising the chassis of the Kübelwagen with Beetle running gear, the Plattenwagen featured a box-like cab positioned directly over the vehicle's rear-mounted engine.

what became one of unitary construction, thanks to the incorporation of two sturdy longitudinal members supported by strong outriggers.

Nordhoff was adamant that series production would commence before the end of 1949, so that the new vehicle would be readily available early in 1950. His personal involvement in the minutia of the project bordered on the obsessive in his determination to present as near-perfect a vehicle as possible. For example, early in November and just days before the Transporter was due to be

↓ The Plattenwagen was a vehicle born out of necessity following the withdrawal of army vehicles from Wolfsburg. It was created by Ivan Hirst for the specific purpose of carrying goods from one part of the factory to another.

launched to the press, Nordhoff gave instructions that the prototype's weight should be reduced to no more than 875kg (1,929lb); his determination to create a unique load carrier and true market leader was unending.

Speaking at the press launch held on 12 November 1949, Nordhoff revealed not only why his new commercial vehicle was ahead of its time, but also why it would continue in that vein for many years to come.

' ... our Volkswagen [Beetle] is a car without compromises, so will our Transporter be without compromises. This is why we did not start from an available chassis, but from the load space. This load space consists of a driver's seat at the front and the engine at the back; this is the clear no-compromise principle of our Transporter. With this commercial vehicle and only with this commercial vehicle, the load space lies exactly between the axles. The driver sits in the front and there is equal weight in the back, due to the engine and the fuel tank; that is the best compromise ... We would have put the engine in the front without hesitation, if it had been the best solution. However, the famous 'cab above the engine' gave such horrendous handling characteristics even when loaded, that we never even considered it. You can tell by looking at the state of the trees in the British Zone how well the British Army lorries, built on this principle, handle on wet roads when they aren't loaded.'

Although the prototype Transporters were straightforward Panel vans, and it was this vehicle that made its tentative debut on the commercial vehicle stage in February 1950, on the trail of an official launch at the Geneva Motor Show the following month, it was always Nordhoff's intention that a whole series of derivatives should be developed. These came in the form of the truly revolutionary Kombi (a forerunner to today's multifarious MPV if ever there was one), the self-explanatory Microbus, the opulent top-of-the-range Microbus Deluxe, the apparent anomaly of a strictly limited (in production terms) ambulance and finally, at least in those early years, the workaday (but expensive to tool-up for) Pick-up.

## The start of the boom

While initial sales of the Panel van were hardly scorching, Nordhoff's policy of diversity paid handsome dividends, with an ever-increasing flow of revenue heading directly back into Volkswagen's development coffers – allowing a vehicle such as the Pick-up to be developed as early as August 1952.

Two further major eventually emerged, while more minor adaptations of the core models made the vehicle the most versatile in Volkswagen's range, and the envy of others. The Double Cab Pick-up, a useful six-seater that retained all the attributes of its Single Cab sibling, made its debut in November 1958, while the High-Roof Delivery Van, a godsend to the clothing trade and glaziers alike, appeared in the autumn of 1961, based on the general specification of the Transporter for the 1962 model year.

Contrary to Nordhoff's assumed concerns regarding capacity, or the lack of it, at Wolfsburg, Beetle sales boomed in the 1950s to such an extent that not only could Volkswagen not keep up with the demand, but also Nordhoff found it necessary to move the Transporter to pastures new and a purpose-built factory for its production at Hanover. Key to this was the lack of additional workers in the vicinity of Wolfsburg. By diverting to Hanover in 1956, a whole new labour pool materialised. Nordhoff took the decision to build a factory at Hanover on 24 January 1955 and it opened its doors for the first time on 9 March 1956. The date is significant in that some have tried to link the introduction of a face-lifted Splitty, a feat that occurred on 1 March 1955, with

← This pre-March 1955 Panel van is finished in Pearl Grey, possibly the second-most popular colour after Dove Blue.

↓ Despite the large engine lid, there was no access to the interior of the vehicle from the rear.

Ideal for camping and family trips.

Always in time for school.

The all-weather bus off to winter sports.

Like the Volkswagen Sedan, the Station Wagon is at home on all continents. The sturdy air-cooled Volkswagen engine functions dependably under the sub-zero climate of the Alaskan Tundra or in the hot sands of the Sahara.

The Volkswagen plant at Hanover, (below) went into operation in 1956. Here, the finest automated machinery combined with traditional German craftsmanship to produce a precision built, finely finished product . . . the Volkswagen Station Wagon. The rise in production figures seen on the chart below tells why it was necessary to build this plant. Year after year, demand required greater production of all models. At present Hanover produces over 400 trucks and station wagons daily. The big home plant at Wolfsburg now produces only sedans. Over 2000 roll off the assembly line there each day.

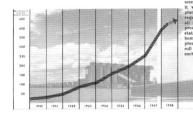

Der VW Kleinbus

The Larger Volkswagen for Large Families and Small Parties

Volkswagen Station Wagon and De Luxe Station Wagon

← Reproduced from Volkswagen publicity material dating from 1958, here is the purpose-built Transporter factory at Hanover, a complex constructed not only to ease the labour situation at Wolfsburg but also to facilitate maximum production of both Volkswagens. The year-by-year daily production figures, rising from under 50 vehicles in 1950 to close on 450 just eight years later, clearly illustrates the demand for Volkswagen's versatile Transporter.

← Throughout the 1950s, Volkswagen's marketing department relied on stylised images of its products to capture the imagination of customers. The artist Bernd Reuters produced a stunning array of artwork of which this example has to be one of the finest. Reuters' style was to elongate and streamline Volkswagen's products, while giving a fleeting but lasting impression of greater speed than might have been possible. Also, by carefully adjusting the scale of the occupants to that of the vehicle, Reuters' artwork implied 'his' vehicles were larger, more opulent and impressive than reality.

← Although the last Reuters' artwork wasn't commissioned until the start of the 1960s, towards the end of the previous decade an increasing reliance had been placed on the work of other artists. Less dramatic and undoubtedly more realistic in nature, this particular cover was designed for the American market. It includes items such as the bullet-shaped indicators and towel-rail bumpers that were not part of the specification elsewhere.

the new factory, whereas in reality, at the time of the change the new building consisted of little more than foundation trenches.

Predictably, Volkswagen's brochure copywriting team used the new factory to the Transporter's advantage: 'Precision built by the finest automated machinery and finished with traditional German craftsmanship, VW Trucks have been so overwhelmingly popular that Volkswagen was obliged to build a brand-new factory in Hanover to keep abreast of the customers' requirements.'

## Promoting the product

As country after country fell to the Beetle's legendary charms of reliability and quality, with the inevitable knock-on effect that afforded the Transporter, clearly there was little or no need to actively market the products to the world. Superbly executed drawings by the artist Bernd Reuters of the Volkswagen family, the Beetle, the Transporter and from 1955, the Karmann Ghia, each skilfully contrived to beautify, elongate and generally add attributes to the vehicles in general, which the Transporter particularly didn't possess. Reuters' artwork was supplemented by a text comparable to that written for other manufacturers; often stilted and contrived by today's standards, but perfectly adequate all those years ago.

The appointment of Carl Hahn (a future director general of Volkswagen AG), as the head of Volkswagen of America in 1959, coupled to the veiled threat of a soon-to-emerge body of US-born and bred would-be usurpers of the Beetle's throne, was sufficient to galvanise the wholly owned subsidiary of the Volkswagenwerk in Germany into action that would not only give tremendous impetus to Transporter sales worldwide, but also change the nature of automobile advertising for ever. Hahn recognised a need that his predecessors, overwhelmed by ever-increasing sales, had overlooked. The day would come when the range would no longer simply sell itself. Promotional gurus, marketing experts and dynamic advertising specialists had to be resourced to maintain the gap between Volkswagen and the rest of the pack. After an intense and wide-ranging interview process, Hahn granted one agency the Beetle portfolio and another, Fuller, Smith & Ross, that of the Transporter.

↑ A pre-March 1955 Microbus with two-tone paintwork. The interior fittings were superior to those of the Kombi. Externally, the Microbus had the same number of windows as its more humble sibling, and a good number less than the top of the range Microbus Deluxe.

↓ Doyle Dane Bernbach (DDB) transformed Volkswagen's image in the United States with a self-deprecating and totally honest style. Gone were picturesque backgrounds and any attempt to portray the Transporter, Beetle and Karmann Ghia in any shape and form other than strict reality. Accompanying pithy text, selling one simple story at a time, proved highly successful.

### Some Volkswagen owners look down on other Volkswagen owners.

When you graduate from a Volkswagen Sedan to a Volkswagen Station Wagon, you really step up in the world.

The Station Wagon stands a good foot taller than other cars.

And it holds more than the biggest conventional wagon you can find.

But the VW Wagon isn't only tall.

It's also short.

We saved 4 feet of hood in front by putting the engine in back.

Big as it is inside, it's only 9 inches longer than the Volkswagen Sedan.

So people who move up to the high-slung model still feel very much at home.

They park in the same little spots.

They still don't worry about freezing or boiling; the engine is air-cooled.

They still go a long way on a gallon of gas (about 24 miles) and a very long way on a set of tires (about 35,000 miles).

And it just tickles them to drive one Volkswagen and look down on a million others.

← This late 1950s Single Cab Pick-up still retaining its original Dove Blue paint is awaiting a full restoration.

↓ The Single Cab Pick-up joined the range of Transporters when sufficient funds had been realised to effect the necessary re-tooling to make such a design possible.

↑ The Double Cab Pick-up was added as a standard part of the Transporter range in 1958. It was not unusual for the military or emergency services to specify such a model, adapted to their own particular needs.

→ The High-Roof Delivery van, which made its debut in the autumn of 1961, was the last major development in model terms, following the introduction of the Double Cab Pick-up in 1958.

While it would be unfair to suggest that the short-lived campaign directed by Fuller, Smith & Ross wasn't effective, it was also apparent that their rivals, the younger and much more vibrant New York-based Doyle Dane Bernbach (DDB) had a distinct edge. A year later, DDB had been granted responsibility for all of Volkswagen of America's products.

One strong storyline per advert, simple, bordering on stark, imagery portraying the Transporter exactly as it was, and pithy text; these were DDB's hallmarks. The thrust behind an advertiser's message had never been so potent.

'That's a load off our front. Now you know why the Volkswagen Station Wagon has that sawed-off look. There is no front in front because we put our engine in the back. The advantages are obvious. The Volkswagen is 4-feet shorter than standard wagons, but only 9-inches longer than the Volkswagen Sedan. It parks like a sports car. Yet inside you can carry more stuff than any wagon made: 1,632lb. Then there are a couple of advantages that aren't so obvious. The VW is nearly a ton lighter on its tires than standard wagons. So 35,000 miles to a set is not unusual. And you'll never need water. Or anti-freeze. The engine's air-cooled. You get the kind of mileage people hope for in compact cars, to say nothing of big wagons. (24mpg is average.) And you're still pushing a hood in front? When all that could be behind you?'

The result of such a message for the Transporter, and for the Beetle too, was that not only did Volkswagen continue to ward off any would-be challenger, but also its products gained an unprecedented cult status both in the automotive world and beyond. The Transporter and the Beetle became icons of the 1960s.

## Summarising the Splitty

During the 17-year lifespan of the first-generation Transporter numerous improvements were made, none more so than in the mid 1950s, when the barn-door engine lid was banished and much improved ventilation was made possible by the introduction of a peak above the windscreen; both changes that rejuvenated the Splitty's appearance. As for the 1960s, consider 1963, a year when extra power was offered to would-be owners in the shape of a 1,500cc engine, and for the '64 model year a much larger tailgate was included, vastly increasing rearward visibility in the process. Finally, 6-volt electrics were banished in favour of modern 12-volt replacements; a move benefiting all final year Splitties. Volkswagen's, for which read Nordhoff's, policy of continual improvement of the product, paid handsome dividends. When the Splitty bowed out in July 1967, 1,833,000 vehicles had been sold, an achievement unparalleled in the world of the small commercial vehicle.

← In its 17-year production run the first-generation model evolved considerably. Its large indicators and the peak over its windscreen easily identify this late example of a Delivery van.

FNB 47T

## Launch of the second generation

↑ The Microbus Deluxe
version of the second-
generation Transporter
changed over the years
(see page 59 for a publicity
shot of the earliest version).
The example shown here
is a special limited edition
that soon became known
as the 'Silver Fish', due to
its metallic silver paint.
Launched in June 1978, this
was the first Transporter to
be offered in a metallic finish.
The eight-seater vehicle was
upholstered in dark blue
cloth, and was endowed with
a long list of extras. It was
only sold in Germany.

The launch of the new Transporter, quickly nicknamed
the Bay thanks to its comparatively panoramic
windscreen when parked side-by-side with the split
screens of its predecessor, had been in the planning
stage since 1964. Its arrival in the summer of 1967
should have lain to rest the oft-trotted out theory
that Nordhoff was incapable of discarding a model
in favour of a genuine replacement. In 1964, Splitty
sales were still increasing year-by-year, but there
was recognition that if Volkswagen was to retain its
lead ahead of its rivals, more than a programme of
continual improvements was necessary. Significant
changes had to be made.

Unlike the rolling agenda of the first-generation
launch, all variations of the second-generation
Transporter were available at once. Admittedly,
the Microbus and Microbus Deluxe had become
the Clipper and Clipper L, borrowed terminology
that would be short-lived when the airline BOAC
realised their flights of the same name had
been compromised. Quickly reinstating the old
terminology, only the Microbus Deluxe suffered
any long-term loss of face and that was unrelated

to a change in name. Sadly, less distinctive than its
predecessor, the Bay version of the Microbus L
maintained the level of luxury it had always been
afforded. Less distinctive though was the metal
sunroof in place of the previous fold-back canvas
affair, as was two-tone paint restricted to a divide on
the roof-line rather than at the waist, while the Bay
range's universal adoption of larger rectangular side
windows, rather than the extra insertion over and
above that of the crowd, a prerogative of the older
Deluxe, left some cold. In summary, the magpie-
attracting bright work of the Splitty Deluxe was still
there in the Bay; it just didn't stand out as well.

The plight of the High-Roof Delivery Van also
merits consideration. Gone were the days of all-
metal construction, as modern glass-fibre definitely
cut down weight, while conceivably being expensive
for Volkswagen to produce.

Despite the intentional hint of cynicism
masking nostalgia for a more costly and sadly less
practical age, the Bay Transporter in its early years
deservedly took sales on to a new plane. That it
was a completely new model is beyond question,
notwithstanding its construction on more-or-less
the same principles as the Splitty and Volkswagen's

brochure copywriters' reference to a face-lifted model. ('The new VW Commercial has had a face-lift. Its looks have been improved.') The engine was new, a 1,584cc unit boasting 47bhp at 4,400rpm. While the top speed of the last Splitty models and the first Bays was virtually the same, the latter had much more in the way of torque at its disposal, ensuring it had to work less hard to produce the result required of it. Swing axles were out, replaced by constant velocity joints and much improved driveshafts. The full list, inappropriate to this brief history, was extensive.

With total first-generation production amounting to in excess of 1.8 million vehicles as already mentioned, it did not come as a surprise when, in 1968, the two millionth Transporter rolled off the production line at Hanover. The Clipper L, finished in Titian Red with a Cloud White roof, didn't find its way into Volkswagen's museum, but was instead donated to a German charity. However, what must have come as something of a surprise to Nordhoff a short time earlier was that his purpose-built factory at Hanover, built to ease the pressure at Wolfsburg, could itself

no longer satisfy the incredible demand for the Transporter, particularly from the United States. As ever, concerned that sales must not be lost, he announced that the Emden plant, which had opened in December 1964 with the primary purpose of building Beetles for the USA, would assist with Bay production. With effect from December 1967, Transporters requiring more finishing than others, in other words the Kombi, Microbus and Microbus L, and which were destined for America, were built at Emden.

Sales of the new Transporter were equally impressive against what increasingly turned out to be alarming times for Volkswagen. From the 253,919 units manufactured in 1968, production peaked at 294,932 vehicles in 1972. The best year for the Splitty had been 1964, but even then this figure fell well short of the Bay's opening score, with 325 Transporters being built over and above a magical 200,000 units. In 1970, 72,515 Bays were exported to the USA alone, while the three millionth Transporter was produced on 3 September 1971. Sadly, for a variety of reasons, this kind of momentum couldn't continue.

↓ Although the Delivery van on the right is a post face-lift version dating from August 1972, it nevertheless serves to illustrate the panoramic nature of the second-generation Transporter's windscreen, nicknamed the Bay window, compared with the split-screen of the first generation.

## Changes at the top

Following the death of Heinz Nordhoff at the age of 69 in April 1968, overall control at Volkswagen passed into the uncertain hands of one Kurt Lotz. Of the few targets he set himself, one appeared to be to rid Wolfsburg and its satellites of the life-blood of the company, the Beetle. With nothing to replace it either available or planned for the near future, this was dangerous ground. Lotz's mercifully short period of leadership (his contract was not renewed after an initial four years as director general), saw Volkswagen's profits tumble from a respectable 319 million DM in Nordhoff's last full year to just 12 million DM when the second director general bowed out against his will.

There then followed four traumatic years for Volkswagen as Rudolf Leiding struggled to develop a new range of water-cooled, front-engine cars out of the mire Lotz had left, and against a background of Europe-wide recession and recurrent oil crises. Profits rallied somewhat, reaching 109 million DM in 1973, before a horrendous result and a 555 million DM loss shook Volkswagen to the core in 1974. Recovery was quick under a further director general, Toni Schmücker, but this was directly due to the new models – Golf, Passat, Polo and Scirocco – instigated by Leiding.

## Later Bay days

While the Transporter had been a crucial money earner for Volkswagen in those difficult years, battered and bruised by the consequences of the oil crises, it became out of step with the newer offerings displayed on Volkswagen's forecourts. Crucially, it was at last seriously challenged by newer, more powerful models emerging from Japan and elsewhere with the result that, in the last four years of its manufacture, sales of the Bay slipped. Although still respectable, particularly when compared with some of the horror stories emerging in other areas of the commercial vehicle

↓ All second-generation Transporters were initially fitted with a 1,600cc single-port engine. With effect from August 1970, this was upgraded to a twin-port, while shortly afterwards first a 1700, then an 1800, and finally a 2.0-litre engine were also offered. The 1600 engine remained an option throughout the years of Bay production.

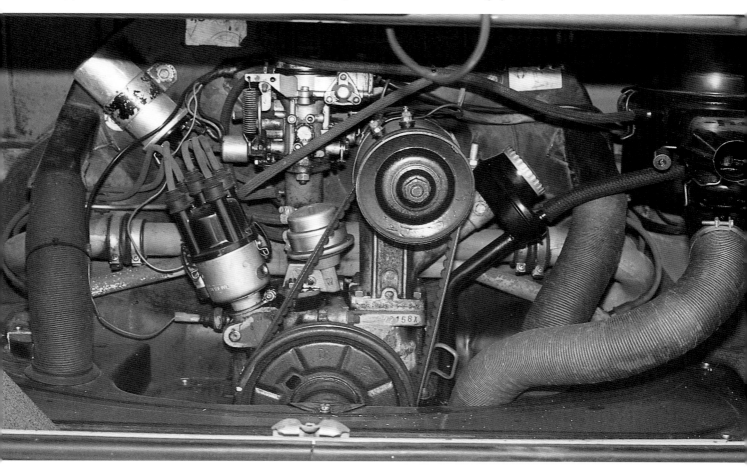

market, the lofty summits of success achieved in the second-generation Transporter's early years were but a distant memory.

Naturally, every effort was made to at least maintain the gap between the Volkswagen product and those of its rivals. One thrust was in the direction of ever-larger engines. After tweaking the single-port 1,600cc into a twin-port, first there was a 1,700cc unit, then a 1,800cc. The arrival of this latter engine in August 1973 at first seemed to be ill-timed at the least, for this was the year of the Arab–Israeli war, of cuts in oil supplies, and almost inevitably of fuel rationing in Britain and many other countries. Manufacturers were looking to produce more fuel-efficient engines, while Volkswagen were increasing the size of theirs. In reality, however, the 1800 had to work less hard to achieve the same result as its predecessor, and while fuel economy could hardly be described as sparkling, it was more frugal than the 1700 in the amount it used. The final increase in engine size for the Bay came in August 1975 for the '76 model year, with a fully-fledged 2-litre offering. By this time Volkswagen was happy to announce a top speed for the Transporter of 80mph (129kph), although many an owner with a 2-litre block at his disposal that had covered a few thousand miles could claim to have made the ton. Undoubtedly more important still was the associated further increase in torque that once and for all laid to rest the fear that the Transporter wasn't up to the job when it came to climbing more than a gentle slope.

At the time the twin-port 1600 engine made its debut, so too did disc brakes, while the fitting of radial tyres on key models helped to keep the Transporter on the road. Would-be owners of '73 models and later Bays, could opt for a three-speed automatic box, a product undoubtedly intended to satisfy the demands of the American market. Fuel injection also became a prerogative of US models, while dual carburettors helped pump up the usable power elsewhere.

Just as the first-generation Transporter underwent a facelift in 1955, so too did the Bay's look alter, although nowhere near as dramatically, this change occurring in August 1972 for the '73 model year. Girder-like bumpers, hidden cab steps and front indicators that were much more visible to oncoming vehicles, summarise the key points of the Transporter's makeover for a modern world.

## Third-generation's surprising specification

When the final second-generation Transporter left the assembly line in the summer of 1979, just 35,000 short of 2½ million Bays had been produced. Nevertheless, the new model was awaited with eager anticipation. A minority of particularly well-informed people were less enthusiastic, for they were aware that when Toni Schmücker had been in post for just a few weeks back in May 1975, he had sanctioned a continuing reliance on air-cooled technology. After all, the argument went, the Bay had no direct competition largely due to its rear-wheel, rear-engined layout. It was easy to point to commercial vehicles with front-wheel drive and their inherent lack of traction, especially in wet weather. Thus, the new model not only sported an out-of-favour, rear-mounted engine like its predecessors, but also all options were of a traditional flat-four, air-cooled, nature; the familiar 2-litre and a rather more irritating suitcase-style version of the long under-powered 1600.

Possibly the third-generation Transporter escaped the wrath of the motoring press for its use of allegedly antiquated technology thanks to its otherwise thoroughly modern design that included such features as light and airily large windows, plus a

↑ **With effect from August 1972, all Transporters (with the exception of the Pick-up initially) fitted with the larger engine could be specified with a three-speed automatic gearbox.**

→ **Once again, all variations, including the Double Cab Pick-up, were available when the third-generation model, nicknamed the Wedge, was launched.**

↘ **Third-generation Transporters destined for the United States were described and badged as Vanagons. The name can be seen on the bottom right section of the vehicle's tailgate.**

↓ **The water-cooled third-generation Transporter, seen here in the guise of a Leisuredrive Camper, can be identified by its double front grille.**

passenger car-style cab. Conceivably the contortions displayed by Volkswagen's copywriters, now so used to surreptitiously condemning the era of air-cooled supremacy in favour of modern water-cooled advances, worked their magic. The following extract appeared in brochures produced for the British market in the early years of the new Transporter's lifespan.

'The first Volkswagen commercial rolled off the production line in March 1950. Since then, the advances in automobile technology made by Volkswagen have set the standard for light commercial vehicles. Now after 4.8 million Commercials, Volkswagen introduce the new Commercials. Volkswagen designers and technicians evaluated the many different drive concepts. They concluded that the best possible layout for this class of vehicle had forward control with the engine behind the rear axle, driving the rear wheels. This drive concept, which has proved to be so successful over the years, has been retained. So too, has Volkswagen's air-cooled engine, renowned for its reliability and durability ...'

Although infinitely more subtle, Volkswagen of America's storyline was equally defensive of air-cooled

↑ **The third-generation Double Cab Pick-up is seen here in syncro guise, and can be easily identified by its high stance.**

technology for the new Transporter, or Vanagon as it was called in the USA and Canada. Perhaps in this instance there was good reason too, for, after an impressive start, the so-called star of the new-generation of water-cooled cars, the Golf, or, in American parlance the Rabbit, had hit the doldrums in sales performance, a situation aggravated by frequent reports of poor build quality and unreliability.

'Thirty-three years ago a pair of small, strange-looking cars appeared on American roads. And almost overnight America discovered Volkswagen made extraordinary cars. Our long history of being at the front of automobile design and innovation is no accident ... [The Vanagon] a fuel-efficient vehicle? ... German engineering experience, synonymous with performance. Performance without compromise. The same Volkswagen know-how that resulted in the design of the Volkswagen Bus originated this totally unique concept in German automotive engineering. The Vanagon. A space saver. A gas saver. And the continuation of a great tradition on the road.'

Praise for the third-generation Transporter at its launch was near universal, as has already been hinted. Larger than its predecessor, but still easily manoeuvrable, much better use had been made of the space available. Three people could sit in

the cab, or at the front of the vehicle in the case of a Microbus, in far greater comfort than had been possible earlier. With a lower rear-loading platform, a floor-pan that encouraged easier access to the vehicle by 100mm, less overall weight due to the removal of a need for the hefty cross-members of old, and even more minor, but appreciated, considerations such as the relocation of the spare wheel to a hinged metal tray under the front of the vehicle, rather than an obtrusive location within the body of the Transporter, perhaps it was inevitable that discrepancies in the use of modern technology could be overlooked.

## T3 or T25 – Commercial Vehicle, Transporter or Bus

The launch of the third-generation model brought a further issue to the forefront, although it was more-or-less overlooked due to the furore caused by the model's layout and method of cooling. In the early days of the 1950s it was easy to accept that the first commercial vehicle and Microbus lacked a name other than the loose one of Transporter. Likewise its model description, the simple designation Type 2 that followed in the footsteps of the Type 1, the saloon,

sedan or Beetle, was straightforward. However, over a decade after the last first-generation model left the assembly line circumstances had changed. While latter-day Beetles had been attributed with badges bearing derivatives such as 1303S and 1200L, the new generation of water-cooled cars sported brand identity and hopefully for the future, loyalty names that ranged from Polo, through to Golf and Passat. These advances were not passed down to the third-generation Transporter.

Ignoring the water-cooled LT range, introduced in April 1975, Volkswagen chose to head their publicity material and brochures with the somewhat bland heading, 'The new commercials from Volkswagen. Transporter. Bus.' As a complication, at least in Germany, the third-generation Transporter was officially designated as the T3. Volkswagen already had a Type 3 buried in its archives in the form of the not-all-that-long-since defunct VW 1500 and 1600 range. This vehicle, launched in 1961 and axed in 1973, was the third distinct style of Volkswagen to be produced after the Beetle and Transporter, hence the designation T3.

Fortunately, this added twist was excused the British, as in the UK the third-generation Transporter

bore the official, if rather half-hearted, recognition tag of T25. North American owners were fortunate in that the adoptive name of Vanagon had become so widely used that Volkswagen there were quite happy to append this name to all literature.

For many years unloved by enthusiasts, as often a 'new' model can be, when Bay and particularly Splitty values started to rocket, the then bargain basement prices asked for the outdated and replaced T3 generated a growing band of followers and the inevitable nickname associated with a cherished vehicle. Thanks to its slab-sided appearance and angular looks, the third-generation Transporter soon became affectionately known as the 'Wedge' and, occasionally, the 'Brick'.

## Third-generation changes direction

For those whose delight in Volkswagen's retention of air-cooled technology was blatantly obvious in 1979, sadly reality meant that their assumed victory was short-lived. Within 13-months of the new model's launch, technicians at Hanover had wedged the diesel engine offered in the Golf from 1976 into the T3, albeit tilted at a 50-degree angle. Another year down the line and water-cooled petrol engines had ousted the last of the air-cooled offerings produced on German soil. For air-cooled fans the only solace to be found was in Latin America, where such methods of cooling survived into the 21st century.

Volkswagen's own historians have consistently made little reference to the sudden change in direction for a vehicle designed specifically for one method of cooling after such a short period in production. Writing in 1990 of the events that occurred just eight years previously, Wolfsburg's Public Relations Department simply stated:

'The Transporter was now fitted with the newly developed water-cooled boxer engines with outputs of 44 and 57Kw*. Consequently all Volkswagens with the exception of the Beetle had water-cooled engines. This was the conclusion of the technical restructuring.'

(*44Kw and 57Kw equates to 60 and 78 DIN bhp respectively.)

Much more recently in 2003, Markus Lupo, writing in the volume entitled *Volkswagen Chronicle – Historical Notes* and guided by Volkswagen's Group Communications, Corporate History Department, failed to note any changes to the T3 Transporter in 1982, but did explain what drove the manufacturer at that time.

'The Japanese export offensive, redirected from America to Europe in 1979, resulted in a competitive situation that could not be won on the price front alone. Volkswagen's strategy was to concentrate on maintaining its technical advantage and increasing the flexibility of its production system in order to improve its ability to react to market change.'

Despite the inevitable costs of building engines suitable for use in just one out of the range of Volkswagen products, the results in terms of both performance and fuel economy went some way to stop the advance of the Japanese manufacturers. With a 20 per cent boost in power and more importantly, at least according to Volkswagen, a 36 per cent increase in torque, not to mention the benefits of up to a further 15 per cent in terms of miles per gallon, so it should have done so too!

Nevertheless, from the 217,876 T3s manufactured in 1980, the first full year of Wedge production, the figure slipped to 155,500 in 1983, the first occasion when the new engines had been under the spotlight for a full 12 months. Although during 1986 production

peaked at 161,712 units, this was still a considerable shortfall compared with the halcyon days of earlier generations. By the time the T3 bowed out in the summer of 1990 manufacture had trickled away to just 370 units over the 130,000 mark. Defenders of the decision to change direction both then and now would undoubtedly argue that if Volkswagen had clung to the traditionally noisier system of cooling, difficult trading conditions would have been further exacerbated, but who knows!

For those charged with convincing would-be purchasers to buy the new models the situation was even more difficult. Having defended air-cooling to the hilt, as evidenced earlier, their job was now to perform a complete U-turn. The solution to the dilemma appeared to praise what was past, while implying a gentle evolution had taken place. Higher standards were evident in 'responsiveness and pulling power', exhibited in 'maximum economy', while engine noise was 'much lower'. There was even a chance to link passenger comfort to the new engines as 'the water-cooled engine enable[d] the heater to respond more rapidly in cold weather ...'

↓ **The most powerful petrol engine fitted in later years to the third-generation Transporter, featured fuel injection and developed 112bhp.**

## New names and models

By the time T3 production ceased (its successor the T4 was launched on 4 September 1990), moves had been made to add a little marketing sparkle to the range of models offered. Gone were the straightforward days of Microbuses and their Deluxe counterparts. After the emergence of special editions such as the top-of-the-range and dutifully luxurious Carat, later incorporated into the general hierarchy of models, publicity material began to be divided between the workaday models such as the Panel van, 'one of the world's most successful one-tonners', the Pick-up and the Double Cab, which were labelled as Transporters and a new name, the Caravelle. To elucidate, a brochure produced in January 1986 for the British market listed three models of Caravelle, the Caravelle C – an ideal Minibus, the Caravelle CL – greater luxury in every detail, and the Caravelle GL – the executive bus, utilising Volkswagen's general designations for differing degrees of luxury, or the lack of it. By the latter months of 1988 this line up had been revised to include four models, only one of which was officially labelled as a Caravelle. Presented in descending order, the Carat was described as 'the executive limousine with space comfort and performance', the Caravelle as providing 'executive transport for seven people', while the Coach a 'general purpose people carrier' and the Bus, a 'perfect base for 12-seat or welfare conversion', followed.

From the relatively humble days of the first water-cooled engines, options that in reality still saw the Wedge lagging somewhat behind the general pace of traffic, Hanover pulled out the plugs and developed a 1.9-litre 78bhp petrol engine, augmented by a 2.1-litre 112bhp fuel injected option. They also boosted the 1.6 diesel up to 70bhp through the addition of a turbocharger, while on offer from 1985, in both Transporter and Caravelle guise, was an all-wheel-drive system branded as the Syncro. Providing automatic monitoring and control of drive to the front wheels, the syncro's viscous coupling made the vehicle ideal for off-road activity where good traction on unmade surfaces was essential. Inevitably, safety reserves were increased in everyday driving too.

With such a line-up both in terms of engine and trim specification, perhaps it was predictable that in the face of strong competition, Volkswagen's publicity machine was prepared to describe its range as 'the new face of Volkswagen'.

**↓ Westfalia campers supplied to America were known as Campmobiles. Such was their popularity in the United States that Westfalia devised specific models geared towards the wishes and desires of American purchasers. A Campmobile is always easy to identify by the American-market orange-and-red side reflectors.**

# The VW Camper?

Although space is dedicated to both the T3's successor and the current T5 elsewhere in this book, as neither model has a big enthusiasts' following yet, the sometimes tangled history of the Transporter is brought to a close conveniently around the 40th anniversary of its launch and the last months of Wedge production, save for one significant issue.

While not every variation of Transporter has been alluded to, if the numerous camper vans based on the three generations, and still seen on the roads today, had been an integral part of Volkswagen's offer, they could hardly have been overlooked. However, as the hopefully familiar names of Devon, Danbury, Canterbury Pitt, Autohome and Autosleeper to mention but a few examples on British roads, and E-Z, Sportsmobile, plus Sundial in America trip off the tongue, realisation should surely dawn that these are conversions by private companies, unlinked to Volkswagen either financially or in any other way. Take Devon to illustrate the point further. As its name might imply, the company had its origins in the south-west of England, when a Sidmouth based joiner and cabinet maker, J P White had the notion of converting Transporters to camping vehicles and selling them through the local Volkswagen dealership.

Undoubtedly, with the camping revolution gathering pace as the 1950s gave way to the 1960s, Transporter sales were encouraged by each operation's use of the Kombi or Microbus particularly, as the base for their respective conversions. In later years, this was further enhanced when a selection of companies became official marketing partners with Volkswagen in the UK and elsewhere.

One independent company above all others became synonymous with Volkswagen and their Transporter, particularly so in Germany and in North America. From tentative steps to produce a removable camping package in the early 1950s, conveniently known as the 'camping box', by the end of the decade North Rhine-based Westfalia's conversions were often included in Volkswagen's brochures and other publicity material. In America this was undoubtedly the case and led to the emergence of terminology as equally contrived as that of Vanagon. Welcome the Campmobile, invariably a straightforward Westfalia offering, complete with identifying decals but, when demand

outstripped supply, a Volkswagen of America, or Volkswagen of Canada, kit designed to mimic the original Westfalia design was sourced and supplied.

Volkswagen's relationship with Westfalia lasted for nearly five decades, encompassing the Splitty, Bay and T3 Wedge central to this book, plus the T4 that followed. However, following Westfalia's acquisition by the Daimler/Chrysler/Mercedes-Benz Group a major problem occurred. Whereas previously Volkswagen had deemed it appropriate to offer Westfalia a preview of each generation of Transporter as it emerged, in order that the company could work on a conversion to suit the van's dimensions, this was certainly no longer the case. Volkswagen would have been offering a rival manufacturer details of their new T5 model before it was launched, something that was obviously out of the question. The solution was for Volkswagen to sever ties and build its own camper in house, which it duly did and launched as the VW California – the first genuine Volkswagen camper in 54 years and five generations of Transporter production.

↑ **The first genuine Volkswagen camper in 54 years, and five generations of Transporter production.**

Compare a pre-March 1955 Transporter of any type with one of the last Splitty models to emerge from Hanover in the summer of 1967 and the differences are immediately evident, and significant. The purpose here is to trace the evolution of the smiley-faced first-generation model in its mainstream guises, from workaday Panel van and Pick-up, via the crossover Kombi, to the forerunner of today's MPV, the Microbus and Microbus Deluxe.

## In the beginning

Although some Panel vans had been produced before March 1950, in order that Volkswagen's most important customers could 'test-drive' the model, what might laughingly be called mass-production started on the eighth of the month at a rate of ten units per day. By the end of the year, 5,662 Panel vans had been built. Although fairly rapidly other paint-colours were made available, in the first nine months of production 3,201 Panel vans were finished in Dove Blue (L31 – Taubenblau), the first colour that would remain synonymous with Volkswagen's commercial vehicle through the era of the Splitty to the Bay and T3 Wedge. The remaining Panel vans produced in 1950 were despatched from the factory in primer, purchasers recognising the advantages of buying a flat-sided vehicle with panels eminently suited to advertising a company's product and displaying its brand colours.

While the original intention had been to build the Transporter on the Beetle's chassis/floor-pan, as outlined in the previous chapter, this was not possible. However, some aspects of the two vehicles were the same, most notable of these being the 25bhp engine. Although in later years there would be criticism levelled at the first-generation Transporter's performance, particularly in terms of its top speed and despite the factory's concerted attempts to boost overall brake-horse-power in 1950, a 25bhp engine was in keeping with the output of other commercial vehicles on offer.

## Panel van launch specification

To enthusiasts, all pre-March 1955 Transporters can be classed as 'barn-door' models, an apt description referring to the extraordinarily large lid at the vehicle's back that gave access to the engine, the 8.8-gallon (40-litre) fuel tank and attendant filler cap, plus the spare wheel. Sadly, the massive door didn't afford access to the Panel van's load space, this being entered by two side-loading doors. Neither did the lid offer any form of engine ventilation system; this was effected by two sets (one each side of the vehicle) of eight outward facing vents.

Initially the spare wheel stood vertically to the right of the cavernous compartment, but from the end of October 1950 it was mounted horizontally on a metal tray above the engine. This move also had the effect of sectioning off the fuel tank filler and part of the pipe from direct contact with the engine; surely a slightly safer arrangement! The filler neck, originally of 120mm diameter was reduced twice in size in the early years, and from March 1953 measured just 60mm.

The relatively small panel above the barn door was simply blank metal, very much in the tradition of smaller commercial vehicles today, although Volkswagen's motive for such a move in 1950 can hardly have been one of the threat of content theft if window glass was added! Until mid-November 1950 an exceptionally large VW roundel adorned the blank panel, but following its deletion it nevertheless took another five months before a small rear window was added. Dedicated early Transporter followers will undoubtedly be aware that early Panel vans lacked a rear bumper, making minor parking damage to the vehicle's rear bodywork much more

← **The first-generation Transporter was produced for 17 years and over 1.8 million examples were built. Today, the Splitty is the most sought after of all Transporters and as a result commands exceptionally high prices. This example has been converted to a camper, having started life as a single colour Kombi and dates from the early 1960s.**

↑ Very few Barn Door Panel vans have survived, primarily due to their purpose in life. Visitors to the Continent will probably have seen both the vehicle pictured here and the one sign-written for Autohaus Lottermann. While a reasonable percentage of Barn Door workhorses left the factory finished in primer, of those that were painted by far the most common colour was Dove Blue, as pictured here.

likely. While, as will be seen shortly, the most upmarket versions of the Splitty acquired a rear bumper quite quickly, it was 21 December 1953 before the Panel van and other first-generation Transporters were so endowed.

Key to the Panel van's success was its neutral handling, a result of the well-balanced design insisted upon by Nordhoff. With the driver and passengers sat over the front wheels and the engine placed aft the rear ones, the cargo space was substantial. Designed to carry goods up to a total weight of 750kg (1,654lb), with 4.6cu m (162.5cu ft) of available space, the self-contained load area was accessed by double doors placed on the opposite side of the vehicle to the driving position. This meant that the vehicle could be unloaded from the kerb without danger from passing traffic. From June 1951 the Panel van could be specified with cargo doors on both sides and in such instances under-floor belly plates were added to retain the vehicle's original rigidity. (For the same reason, the plates were also a feature of any model with a sliding canvas sunroof.) Initially with no division other than the bulkhead between the cab and the load area, from 16 June 1950 this area became completely sealed from the driver and passenger compartment by a hardboard

panel above the bulkhead. However, with effect from 20 April 1951 a small observation window was inserted, not only giving a view of the goods stored in the rear but, more importantly, allowing the driver rearward vision to the new window cut in the rear panel. The loading area was unlined and two steps were taken in the early days to reduce condensation. In November 1950, three outward facing air vents were cut into either side of the top rear side panels, while two months later the load area panelling was sprayed with an anti-condensation agent.

The Panel van's cab was simplicity itself. A single, unadjustable bench seat, lightly padded and covered in a fine-grain vinyl accommodated three people, but made no concession to the driver with extra long, or unusually short arms and legs. Plain fibreboard panels were screwed to the doors and front panel, while the headlining, if it can be called such, was made of simple hardboard. The floor was covered in a single-piece, horizontally ribbed, rubber mat. Passengers were granted a painted foot bar and grab-handle, while the driver steered the vehicle with a near-on-horizontal commercial-vehicle-type three-spoke steering wheel, finished in black. The handbrake was a close-to-vertical affair, as less unusually was the gearlever. The foot pedals were similar to those on the Beetle, making it impossible to use the heel-and-toe style of smooth operation. The floor was also home to the dipswitch, while the metal panel below the bench seat housed both the choke and the rotary knob control for the heater. The remaining instrumentation, such as it was, was housed in a single body-coloured binnacle, with central black section, and was positioned directly in front of the steering wheel.

The speedometer was calibrated to 80kph (50mph), or the vehicle's maximum speed, and to modern eyes appeared to run backwards, until it was revised in December 1953. Two switches, to the left and right of the speedometer, operated the wipers and headlamps respectively. Warning lights to indicate the semaphores (red) and headlamps (blue) were on the left, while on the right at the top was one to denote ignition (red) and below it one for oil pressure (green). The ignition switch was placed centrally between the two switches already referred to, while on the left side of the binnacle there was a separate starter button. A toggle switch to the top right of the binnacle operated the semaphores.

Sliding rather than wind-down side windows have been deemed to be a cost-cutting measure, while ventilation was improved by piano-hinged swivelling quarter-lights. As this issue still caused some owners cause for concern, with effect from March 1953 the aftermarket Behr air scoop became available as a service part. Finally, the driver only was provided with a grey fibreboard sun-visor.

At its front, a pre-March 1955 Panel van was distinguishable by a stylish crease at the forward end of the roof, with a rain gutter being the only break in the lines before the distinctive split panes of the windscreen. A large VW roundel, initially made of cast aluminium, dominated the look of the vehicle. From April 1951, a crisper design of painted-steel roundel with a linked V and W of Volkswagen's marque designation was introduced. The bumper had a broken central convex pressing, the part without a pressing being allocated to the vehicle's registration plate, and extended in front of the lower valance and below the cab doors. The semaphore indicators were located immediately in the metalwork behind the side windows of the cab.

↓ **This dramatic image of an early Transporter shows the lack of ventilation slots above the split screens. This was one of the reasons why the original Transporter was restyled in March 1955.**

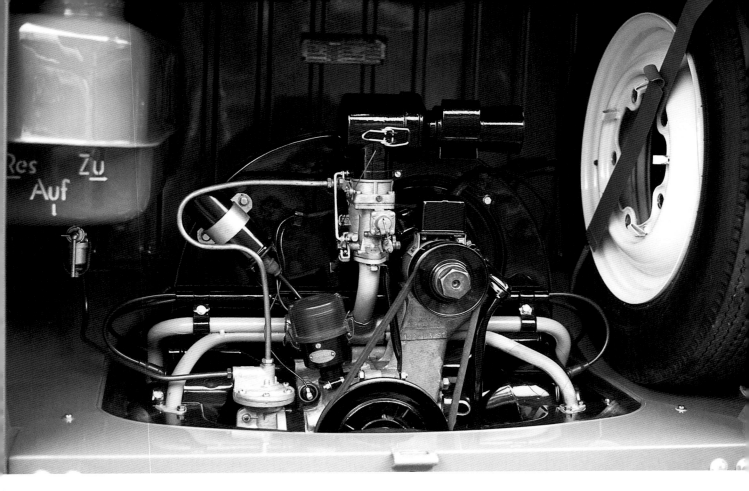

All first-generation Transporters had a 6-volt
electrical system until the last year of production,
while originally, the Panel van and its brethren ran on
16in wheels and tyres. Front suspension was by means
of transverse torsion bars, parallel trailing arms and
telescopic dampers. At the rear similar use was made
of torsion bars, trailing arms, and telescopic dampers.
Swinging half axles completed the story. Until March
1953, the gearbox was of the non-synchromesh
variety, while reduction boxes, that had first seen
daylight in the Porsche-designed wartime Kübelwagen,
were fitted to address the Panel van's lethargic
performance when fully laden. Amazingly, reduction
boxes remained a feature of all first-generation
transporters to the end of production in July 1967.
Unlike the Beetle, which came with cable brakes until
the spring of 1950, the Transporter was fitted with
hydraulic brakes from the start.

The same 1,131cc air-cooled, flat-four engine that
had been in use in the Beetle since 1943 powered
the Panel van at launch. Bore and stroke stood at
75mm and 64mm respectively, with the maximum
output of 25bhp being developed at 3,300rpm. To
take into account the wide variation in the quality
of fuel available across Europe at the time, the

compression ratio was set at a lowly 5.8:1. Initially
a Type 26VFI or VFJ downdraught carburettor was
fitted, although by the start of 1953 this had been
replaced by a Solex 28PCI. Although Volkswagen
quoted the official top speed as a gentle 50mph
(80kph), in reality 55mph (88kph) was easily
achievable. Acceleration through the gears from
rest to 40mph took some 22.7 seconds, while a
fully laden Panel van would struggle to accelerate
between 25mph (40kph) and 50mph in less
than 80 seconds. Fuel consumption, as might be
imagined, was relatively heavy at around 25mpg
(11 litres/100km) average, something that would
remain a feature throughout the production run
of the first two generations of Transporter and
in many instances well beyond. In the 1950s,
Volkswagen was nevertheless proud of the
vehicle's achievements in this field when compared
with the competition.

To conclude the summary description of the
Panel van at launch, here is a short extract from
a brochure published for the American market
a few years into Transporter production: 'It is
the ultimum (sic) in low-cost transportation. Just
think of it, it can haul a full load at 50mph over

← With effect from November 1950, the prominent VW roundel on the panel above the Transporter's large engine lid was discontinued, although at that stage it wasn't to make way for the insertion of a rear-window. Early vehicles lacked a rear bumper.

↓ This image more than any other indicates why the early Transporters were nicknamed 'Barn Doors'!

→ The Behr air-scoop (MO93) was a popular optional equipment item in the days of the pre-March 1955 Transporter. As the name implies, the air-scoop was a means to improve cab air-circulation. When Volkswagen redesigned the front of the Splitty in 1955, a ventilation system was created that negated the need for an air-scoop.

↓ Although this is by no means an early example of a Kombi, the appearance of the vehicle nevertheless identifies it as a more basic Transporter. Note particularly the painted wheels and the lack of chrome.

a mile on only the equivalent of 1½ cocktail glasses of gasoline! Furthermore, it is a bear for punishment. You can put three shifts of drivers on a Volkswagen Transporter and operate it day and night without harming it. More than half a million Volkswagen drivers know that its running expenses are less than those of any other car in the world. All it requires is surprisingly little gasoline and every 1,200 miles a small can of oil and standard servicing. Such a vehicle is your best business partner.'

## The Kombi – a significant development

A further two options were available within just over two months of the official March 1950 launch of the Panel van, proving that it had always been Nordhoff's intention to evolve a family of Transporters. The first of the two by a matter of a few days, the Kombi, made its debut on 16 May and proved to be one of the most significant vehicles to emerge from Wolfsburg, or its future satellites, for many a year.

The Kombi benefited from three significant differences to the Panel van specification in the form of both additional windows and seats, but minus the full-height partition between the cab and 'loading' areas. Other than that, it was more or less identical to its lowlier brother.

Clearly, as the Kombi was designed to offer both light and seating in the area specifically allocated to load carrying in the Panel van, it was inappropriate to retain the hardboard panel above the bulkhead and this was summarily removed.

Three almost square windows were cut into either the panels, or loading doors, down each side

of the vehicle, leaving an unequal expanse of painted metal towards the Kombi's rear. Although to those familiar with the Kombi's appearance there is nothing unusual in that, the original purpose was to form an enclosed luggage storage compartment over the engine, bearing in mind that early vehicles lacked any form of rear window. Artist Bernd Reuters, whose wonderful stylised interpretations of all models of Volkswagen were used extensively in brochures and other promotional material throughout the 1950s, depicted the Kombi with elongated, or rectangular, side windows, the effect being to make the vehicle look more streamlined than it was in reality.

Two rows of easily removable seats were added to the Panel van specification. Constructed on a simple steel framework very much in the same way as those in the cab, the seats were covered in identical vinyl material, although they benefited from slightly deeper and better-padded cushions. Standing on tubular steel legs they could be easily attached and removed from the floor by simply screwing or unscrewing conveniently large wing nuts. The standard specification was one of two three-seat benches, the one opposite the side loading doors benefiting from a separate tipping backrest for the section closest to

the doors, thus making access to the rear bench much easier. However, a lower cost option was to stipulate a two-seat bench opposite the side loading doors, although this inevitably reduced the vehicle's overall seating capacity. Volkswagen was quick to point out that the middle bench could be removed while the rear one was still available for passenger usage if a smaller load was to be carried. Finally, as a factory-fitted option and given the code M57 at least until March 1955, the Kombi could be supplied with divided front seats, making it a walk-through affair allowing easy access to the storage or passenger area at the expense of one seat in the cab area. Here then was flexibility personified.

The floor, which was simply bare metal in the Panel van, was covered in ribbed rubber, but that was about the only gesture towards any form of passenger comfort. The Kombi lacked any headlining in the rear and was devoid of even basic panelling below the waistline, while around the windows bare metalwork was only too apparent. Although a good percentage of 1950's owners and passengers would have found such a state of affairs acceptable, for those with more money to spend, the Microbus entered production with effect from 22 May 1950.

**↑ The success of the Kombi lay in its versatility. Primitive it might seem, but by undoing simple wing nuts a Kombi owner could remove as many seats as they wished, thus creating either a partial or full van. Kombi floors were clad with hardwearing rubber and there was a complete lack of any form of door card, or other interior trim, in the passenger area.**

## The Microbus – 'an oversize passenger car'

Volkswagen's publicity machine was eager to educate potential Microbus purchasers that what they were buying was an 'oversize passenger car accommodating eight people.' The broadcast message deliberately omitted references to the vehicle's load carrying abilities and to its handling characteristics when fully laden.

Even before peering through a window of the earliest Microbus, it was possible to distinguish some of its number from the Kombi, for the model that would have transitory top-of-the-range status could be purchased with two-tone paintwork. Although the only reference to paint colours to date has been of Volkswagen's ubiquitous Dove Blue and the option to buy a vehicle merely coated with primer, both the Panel van and Kombi were soon offered in other shades. Until the end of February 1953 these comprised two shades of grey, both Pearl and Medium, plus Chestnut Brown and Brown Beige. The Microbus, on the other hand was launched in straightforward Stone Grey, or with Brown Beige upper panels and Light Beige lower ones.

Inside, the Microbus featured a full-length woollen headlining, with matching material fixed around the side windows. Below the waistline the interior was clad with fibreboard panelling that extended to the side loading doors. Two substantial grab-handles were fitted to the bulkhead partition, (one horizontal and the other vertical, close to the side loading doors), while the bench seat opposite the doors also sported a grab handle for the use of the occupants of the rear bench. Initially the first-mentioned bench seat was designed for two occupants, leaving space for access to the rear of the vehicle, but this was soon extended to a full three-seat bench, with a tilting back section closest to the door. All the seats were covered in vinyl, which was better padded than that of the Kombi, while also being pleated and piped for a more luxurious look.

A proliferation of chrome fittings, coat hooks, ashtrays and interior light fittings likewise marked out the Microbus from the Kombi, while some of the earliest examples featured a partitioned luggage compartment with a vertical sliding shutter over the engine compartment. Finally, the rear window of each set of three down the vehicle's side could be opened on a chrome catch.

With effect from February 1956, a seven-seater version of the Microbus supplemented the standard nine-seat offering.

↓ **The pre-March 1955 Microbus can be easily identified by the lack of a peak above the split screen. The vehicles were available either in two-tone paintwork as shown, or in a single colour finish. In this instance, the colour options appear to be unique to the vehicle, while the indicators are a later addition. The eagle-eyed may be able to spot the semaphore housings behind the door on the 'B' pillar.**

## The Microbus Deluxe

Spurred on by encouraging and ever mushrooming Beetle figures, burgeoning Transporter sales, and a general upsurge in the German economy, a genuinely upmarket version of the Microbus was previewed at the Frankfurt Motor Show in April 1951, before going into full production two months later. This version of the Transporter, officially the Microbus Deluxe, but known for many years in enthusiast circles at least as the Samba, encompassed many unique features and as a consequence commanded a premium amounting to 20 per cent more than the price of the Microbus. Volkswagen's marketing of the new product seemed to have been almost exclusively directed towards the company buyer, rather than private individuals. Bernd Reuters was duly commissioned to produce artwork depicting the Samba delivering people to airports, railway stations and grandiose hotels, while brochure text was similarly geared to luxury transport.

'This airline uses Volkswagen MICRO BUSES DE LUXE because it wants to give passengers maximum comfort and economy of transport. No words or

pictures can properly convey to you the beauty, comfort and numerous advantages of this remarkable eight-passenger vehicle.'

Unlike the Microbus, and for that matter the Kombi, the Samba sported four windows on each side of the vehicle behind the side cab ones. Additionally, four oblong skylights sat along the vehicle's length at either side. The first of these was positioned over the cab door, while the last sat above the third window along each side of the vehicle. Curved by the nature of their position in relation to the roof's contours, the skylights were made of material marketed as Plexiglas, similar in nature to Perspex and at the time in use in the production of aeroplane canopies. Plexiglas was also used to glaze two wraparound windows in the rear quarter-panels. Compared with the rest of the range, the Microbus Deluxe's rear window was considerably larger, leaving slim pillars of metal between it and the surrounds for the Plexiglas panes. As if all these windows, a total of 23, including the front and rear screens, weren't extravagant enough, the Samba also came with a Golde full-length and fold-back canvas

↑ **The Microbus Deluxe was by far the most costly version of the first-generation Transporter, but in its fittings and trim it was also superior to the rest of the range. Note particularly the fold back canvas sunroof, Plexiglas skylights and the delightful rear quarter windows. Tally them up and the total comes to an astonishing 23, making the vehicle both light and airy.**

sunroof. (Volkswagen's policy regarding sunroofs in the 1950s, and to a certain extent 1960s, appears odd to modern eyes, for not only could a sunroof be fitted to the Microbus, but also to the Kombi, just as with the Beetle purchasers could opt to buy the basic standard model likewise endowed.)

Apart from its distinguishing window structure, the Microbus Deluxe was also home to a long catalogue of bright work trim. Starting at the vehicle's front, the Samba boasted a chromed VW roundel compared to the other Transporters' painted version. Polished mouldings adorned the 'V'-shaped swage lines and these continued down the side of the body under the side windows and across the vehicle's rear in a never-ending circle. The front bumper sported rubber strips encased in bright work mouldings. Further polished bright work linked the two sets of wheels, being attached to the outside of the sills. At the rear, although a fully protective bumper wasn't fitted initially, trim strips, similar in nature to the design of the front bumper, protected the rear quarter panels, leaving just the barn door vulnerable to knocks. From March 1953, the Samba was fitted with a full rear bumper, identical in its make up to the front one, and several months ahead of the rest of the range, which had to wait until December of the same year to be so adorned. Inevitably, chrome hubcaps were standard, the centre VW symbol being painted in the lower body colour of the vehicle.

Like the Microbus, the Samba was available with either two-tone paintwork, or a single shade. The single colour of Stone Grey was the same as that of the Microbus, but the two-tone option of Chestnut

← (Top) Although this image is of a later 21-window Microbus Deluxe, rather than the earlier 23-window version, there is still an overwhelming feeling of light and airiness. Note the 'jail bars' fitted to the rear luggage compartment to prevent items hitting the glass.
(Middle) Although the Microbus Deluxe in first-generation form could be specified without a canvas pull-back sunroof, it is this feature, manufactured by Golde, that epitomised the luxury nature of the vehicle.
(Bottom ) The interior of the Samba was luxuriously appointed and for many years featured two-tone trim. Unlike the more basic people carriers, the side walls of the interior were also trimmed, while chrome fitments were in abundance. The curious bulge with a shelf on top, positioned on the partition between the cab area and the passenger compartment, concealed the spare wheel.

Brown over Sealing Wax Red produced a colour combination that many an enthusiast has chosen to copy with their own vehicle many years later. When the colour options were reviewed in March 1955, and in most cases amended, the Chestnut over Sealing Wax option remained on the list, and survived there until July 1958.

Inside, the Samba was equally luxurious. A full headlining, additional lights, ashtrays and chromed fittings are taken for granted, but in the cab, Volkswagen went to some length to offer a cut-above-the-rest package. While the three-spoke steering wheel was finished in ivory rather than black, an attribute passed across from Deluxe Beetles produced from 1949 onwards, the Samba also sported its own exclusive full-length metal dashboard, painted in the lower body colour, and complete with ivory surrounds to the fittings. While the basic equipment was more or less the same as that housed in the single binnacle of the rest of the range, the Samba had a large clock opposite the passenger closest to the door, plus a central blanking panel, complete with an impressive VW logo, that could be home to an extra-cost radio if so wished. A chromed ashtray that sat in front of the clock and

closer to the split screens completed the package.

Pleated and piped upholstery throughout, superior trim panels and ivory-coloured fittings in the body of the Samba were complemented by a carpeted luggage area that was surrounded by chromed rails introduced to stop cases slipping and breaking the window glass. Chrome runners protected the carpet and a further raised rail prevented luggage falling on rear-seat passengers.

Compared with the Microbus, Samba sales were always much lower. For instance, in 1952 4,052 of the former were produced, weighed against 1,142 examples of the Deluxe. In 1964, the year when the highest number of all first-generation Transporters was produced, 14,031 Sambas left Hanover, compared with 40,115 Microbuses. Curiously, the last full year of Splitty production was also the best for the Samba, with 18,790 such models leaving Hanover. Conversely, Microbus figures had slumped to 30,767 units.

Finally, it was possible to specify the Microbus Deluxe without a Golde sunroof and the eight Plexiglas skylights. This option, which even had its own model number, was rarely requested and very few such examples survive today.

**↑ The Microbus Deluxe, as launched in June 1951, looked different to this example in that in August 1963 the size of the tailgate and rear window was enlarged. The result was that there was no longer room to accommodate the two rear corner windows. Enthusiasts distinguish between an early and late Microbus Deluxe by referring to them respectively as a 23- or 21-window model.**

## The Ambulance

Volkswagen's Krankenwagen, or Ambulance, sold steadily, albeit in small numbers, throughout the Splitty era. Launched in December 1951, Volkswagen's design team modified the 'barn door' engine lid and rear panels to accommodate a tailgate through which a stretcher and patient could be loaded and unloaded.

After a good number of years devoted to the Volkswagen marque, it still never fails to surprise that the Ambulance was regarded as an integral part of the Transporter range. Evidence, in the form of a factory memo dating from as early as August 1949, indicates that the Ambulance was one of the planned second-stage prototypes to be built, and that only Nordhoff's impatience to present the Panel van to the world's press in November prevented this. Once the Ambulance had joined the other options already launched, its likeness, in the form of Reuters' artwork, was included in most if not all sales literature for many years, while text detailing its attributes was also added. It can only be assumed that Volkswagen was not expecting customers to ponder whether they should buy a Kombi or an Ambulance to fulfil their daily needs, but instead were demonstrating the undeniable adaptability of the Transporter. Such a motive ties in nicely with an ever-expanding range of special models, details of which are covered in Chapter 6.

The Ambulance, or to give it its German name, the Krankenwagen was introduced on 3 December 1951, and designated the type code T27. Previously, or at least from November 1950, the Bonn-based coachbuilder, Miesen, had been converting Transporters to ambulances, just as they had also adapted Beetles for use by the medical service. Externally, at least from the front and the side, the Ambulance bore a strong resemblance to the Kombi and Microbus, although a convenient foot-operated retracting step under the side doors was both standard equipment, and visible to casual observers. A roof-mounted flashing light and three-quarter-height frosted side windows were also giveaways, but it was from the rear that the Ambulance was completely different to any other model in the range.

As a project jointly developed with the experts in the German Ambulance Service, it was quickly recognised that loading patients on stretchers through the two side doors was hardly ideal. It would be much better to slide them in at the rear. To accomplish this, the barn door was abandoned in favour of a much smaller engine lid, and by inference a precursor to modifications that would materialise in March 1955. With both the engine lid and its attendant compartment reduced in size, the fuel filler moved to the loading doors side of the vehicle and was accessed via a D-shaped flap, while the spare wheel relocated to a vertical position behind the cab backrest. It then only remained to create an opening rear hatch, through which two stretchers could be guided into the body of the vehicle to lie side-by-side. A substantial tailgate, hinged at the bottom and supported by chains therefore completed the exterior's unique make-up and, as this obviously lacked a window, took the vehicle in some ways back to the earliest days of Transporter production, while also looking forward to the amendments that would be made to all models in March 1955.

Out of sight, the Ambulance had stronger torsion bar springing, while inside, apart from the two stretchers already referred to, there were two casualty chairs, one of which was designed to be portable and could be eased into the vehicle through the side doors on runners. Roller blinds were provided for the side windows, which were also protected by bars similar in style to those used on the Samba. A buzzer arrangement was fitted so that communication could be maintained with the driver, who sat in front of a full height partition into which had been cut a full-width window, consisting of separate sliding glass panes. An electrically operated fresh air ventilator was fitted to the centre of the roof panel, while both the headlining and side panels were made of easily wiped-clean materials. The remainder of the equipment supplied was even more specialist to the needs of the ambulance service.

In 1952, the first full year of manufacture, 481 Ambulances left Wolfsburg, with 1965 proving to be the year when more such vehicles were required than any other in the first-generation's 17-year production run. To put the matter into perspective, in 1952 the Ambulance accounted for just over two per cent of total manufacture, while by 1965 even that figure had dropped to just less than half a per cent of overall production.

## The Pick-up

Although an unquestionable asset to the Transporter range, the Pick-up made its debut as late as the end of August 1952 and with very good reason. Unlike the developments required to produce each successive variation, including the Samba for which a premium price could be charged anyway, the basic design of the Transporter required extensive revision for it to be successfully launched as a Pick-up. Such re-tooling was an expensive business and it was only when Nordhoff was happy that sufficient resources could be spared that the green button for the Pick-up was pressed.

With a flatbed as the key element in its make-up, the normal barn door engine lid, and attendant voluminous space for the engine, petrol tank and spare wheel, was out of the question. Fortuitously, a practical and logical position for the spare wheel had already been established when the Ambulance's tailgate requirements demanded a relocation. Similarly, there was a precedent for the relocation of the fuel-filler. However, what hadn't been necessary previously was a new design of fuel tank. The new and flatter tank was located above and to the right of the gearbox, which in turn resulted in a fuel filler door positioned well in front of the vehicle's rear wheels. The engine's cooling vents, still facing outwards and eight in number per bank, were cut into the side panel behind the rear wheelarches. A new panel to act as a cab roof also had to be pressed, while the metalwork creating the cab's rear wall had built-in strengthening convex pressings on both sides of the space for a small rear window.

The flatbed was made out of two equal-sized sheets of metal, which were corrugated for strength and protected by 15 hardwood strips, fixed

↓ The Pick-up could only be launched when sufficient funds had been amassed to pay for the necessary changes and re-tooling required to the basic first-generation model. This particular example dates from 1965, but the first Pick-ups appeared in late August 1952. Comparatively few Pick-ups have survived, undoubtedly a result of their workhorse nature.

This Pick-up dates from 1961 and is finished in Dove Blue, L31, the most popular shade of all for Volkswagen's workhorse vehicles. Assembled at the Clayton factory in Australia, as this is a CKD (completely knocked down) kit, rather than a vehicle manufactured in a satellite operation, it is virtually identical to the product built at Hanover. Note the pristine hood and bows, and the under-floor storage area suitable for valuables, as its contents were concealed from prying eyes and its door could be locked.

longitudinally with the dual purpose of protecting the metalwork from near inevitable damage, while hinting at a degree of extra stiffness to the structure as well. Both the rear and side-flaps were robust affairs. However, their use by members of the building trade, and others, in the early days suggested that it would be wise to add four rectangular pressings per side flap and three to the tailgate for even greater rigidity. This improvement came into effect in November 1953. The side flaps were fitted with eyes for an extra-cost tarpaulin, while rubber stops attached to all the flaps prevented metal clashing with metal, with the inevitable damage that would have been sustained by the lower panels.

The Pick-up offered purchasers 4.2sq metres (45sq ft) of flatbed loading space, but Volkswagen's designers had more to offer. The problem appeared to be one of getting that message across. Early marketing material might have looked wonderful and Reuters once again produced a first-rate interpretation of the workaday Pick-up, but frequently, and certainly in this instance, the accompanying sales text appeared both staid and clumsy. A key message concerning the

Pick-up was the ingenious use of all available space, which, as far as the copywriter was concerned, meant: 'The Volkswagen Pick-up Truck has what others do not – a lower compartment.' Below the flatbed and between the two sets of wheels, Volkswagen had ingeniously created a secure and dry storage area amounting to a floor area of 1.9sq metres (20sq ft). Accessed by a lengthy door with two top hinges on the right-hand side of the vehicle, this was an ideal place in which to store either valuables or heavy items. In the case of the latter, the location between the wheels meant that the Pick-up's handling was unaffected when it was in motion. Volkswagen even thought to ventilate the space with three outward facing vents cut into the door.

The expense involved for Volkswagen in creating the Pick-up proved well worthwhile, with excellent sales figures from the start and throughout the first-generation Transporter's production years. With the launch of the Pick-up, Nordhoff had fulfilled his initial wish list of Transporter options, and while each choice was subject to continual improvement from the day of its launch, the pace seemed to increase as the 1950s developed. If a strict chronology were to be applied, an increase in engine power, production relocation and a major bodywork overhaul would

be the next topics for discussion. However, as Nordhoff and his team were to produce two more distinct Transporter variations over the course of the next decade, logic decrees that these should take precedence in an attempt to conclude the full story of the Splitty family.

## The Double Cab Pick-up

With effect from the final months of 1953, the Binz Karosserie started to produce a double-cab Pick-up that became available through VW dealerships as part of the Special Model, or Special Equipment package, (See Chapter 6). Volkswagen supplied normal Pick-ups finished in primer, which the coachworks then adapted. The rear section of the cab was cut off, moved back by some 850mm, (33½in). A new roof panel, third door and new bulkhead section were created to complete the new cab, while the original side flaps were cut, shortened, and re-welded to take into account the extra space now taken up by the elongated cab. The extended cab's windows were bigger than the standard Volkswagen offering, but were sealed units, while the new cab door opened in the suicide

↓ **This Double Cab Pick-up didn't leave the factory with the two-tone finish it has now. All such vehicles were only available with single colour paint. Only US models featured towel-rail style bumpers. The vehicle's relative youth in Splitty terms can be determined by the larger 'fish-eye' indicators.**

style. Although it is likely that only around 600 Binz double-cabs were built, interest in it was sufficient to stimulate Volkswagen into building its own Double Cab model.

In late September 1958, Volkswagen added both a wide metal bed and a wooden bed version of the Pick-up. Both came in direct response to demands made on them by the building trade in particular. On 3 November, the VW Double Cab Pick-up was added to the model list, and while its specific model number irrevocably linked it to the Single Cab Pick-up, promotional material adopted equal portions of space to both variations.

Volkswagen made more or less the same changes to the Pick-up that Binz had previously, but their model naturally lacked the evidence of cutting and welding apparent in the coach-built version. A longer roof pressing was developed, as was a door giving access to the rear seats. Unlike the Binz affair, Volkswagen's opened like a conventional one, while its window, and the matching one on the other side of the vehicle, were of a more standard size. Sadly, the storage space under the flatbed was lost, but,

by way of compensation, there was room for tools at least under the rear bench seat in the cab.

As Volkswagen's marketing became slicker, the Double Cab Pick-up was frequently referred to as a cross between the Kombi and the Single Cab Pick-up, offering a flatbed load area of 30sq ft and seating for six. There was even the Kombi-like option of removing the rear cab seat, and what by now was being referred to as the 'tool chest' beneath it, when there was a need to carry bulky items under cover, while still transporting up to three people! Such was the inventiveness of the marketing department that it wasn't unusual to hear the vehicle being referred to as the 'Crew Cab', thereby subconsciously reinforcing the people-carrying message.

## The High-Roofed Panel van

Just as the Double Cab was a development of the standard Pick-up for the specific purpose of transporting more people, so too was the High-Roof, this time offering such bodies as the clothing trade,

↓ **The High-Roofed Panel van was the last major addition to the range of Transporters, first appearing in the autumn of 1961. The vehicle proved particularly popular with the clothing trade and the German Post Office.**

glaziers and even the German Post Office the extra height they often required to make their Panel van deliveries effective.

Launched in September 1961, the differences between the High-Roof and the standard Panel van were strictly limited to an increase in the size of certain panels in the case of the new option. As such, the side loading doors were taller, as were the adjoining side panels. The sections over the cab were similarly extended, but the tailgate remained standard, the insertion of an additional panel over it completing the story. Although incurring a weight penalty due to the extra metalwork involved, Volkswagen ruled out the notion of replacing the metal roof with a lighter weight glass-fibre affair.

The High-Roof stood 2,285mm (90in) tall, compared with the standard model at 1,925mm (75.8in). The attendant weight penalty of the additional metalwork that made the High-Roof what it was amounted to 40kg (88lb), but load space between the standard Panel van at 4.8 cubic metres (170cu ft) and the High-Roof's 6.0cu m (212cu ft) made the price in performance terms well worthwhile for many.

↑ A rear-view picture of an early Transporter, complete with large VW roundel, confirms its build date as being before November 1950. Note the now seriously outmoded lighting arrangements. The single fitting over the number plate housed the brake light. The two-chromed bezels contained the night driving lights, but the single reflector was housed separately below and to the left of the vehicle.

## Year-by-year specification revisions 1950–March 1955

At the risk of repetition, some of the specification revisions already having been referred to in the above summary of the models of the first-generation Transporter range, what follows is a summary of the key changes made to the Splitty before the watershed month of March 1955.

### 1950

From 16 June, a partition was added above the bulkhead in the Panel van, dividing the cab from the loading area. As the Panel van (and other models in the range) did not have a rear window, the hardwood partition lacked any form of cut-out that would have allowed a view of the cargo area and the rear of the vehicle.

On 11 September, Panel vans received three outward-facing vents, set as high as possible in each side of the load area and close to the rear of the vehicle, to improve ventilation of the cargo area.

Transporters built on or after 31 October featured the spare wheel mounted on a tray above the engine within the spacious compartment behind the barn door. Previously, the wheel had stood vertically, strapped in place by a leather belt, at the right-hand side of the engine. Transporters built after 11 November no longer sported the large VW roundel on the rear panel that had been a feature from the beginning of production.

### 1951

With effect from 10 April, the VW roundel at the Transporter's front became more precise in its styling as steel was used, rather than aluminium.

All models received a small rear window from 20 April, more or less centrally positioned in the previously blank panel above the barn door engine compartment lid. The length of the two sets of three air vents in the Panel van was increased on 3 August.

### 1952

So that the Transporter might be detected more easily at night, when the lights weren't on, two red reflectors were fitted to the rear of vehicles built on or after 31 March, compared with the previous single reflector at the vehicle's left-hand side. From 11 July, the external mirror arm was mounted to point downwards instead of upwards. The filler neck diameter was reduced from 120mm to 80mm from 4 August.

## 1953

The previous style of quarter-light with a piano hinge-style of operation was replaced by one with a swivelling movement on pins at both the top and bottom. Additionally, the length of the handbrake lever was increased. A 28 PCI carburettor replaced the 26 VFIS version, all changes occurring on 2 January.

The Samba received a full rear bumper on all models built on or after 10 March. At the same time all models were fitted with synchromesh on second, third and top gears.

The Pick-up's side flaps and tailgate received rectangular strengthening pressings; four for the former and three for the latter, with the change occurring on 11 November. A deluge of improvements occurred on 21 December. These included one key to operate the door lock and ignition, a conventional speedometer calibrated to 100kph (previously 80kph) replacing the apparently backward style unit, a combined ignition and starter switch, and the fitting of a rear bumper to the Panel van, Kombi and Microbus. Most important of all though, was a new engine: the 30bhp unit.

| 30BHP ENGINE | |
|---|---|
| Capacity | 1,192cc |
| Bore and stroke | 77mm x 64mm |
| Compression ratio | 6.1:1 (December '53 – April '54) |
| | 6.6:1 thereafter |
| Maximum power | 30bhp at 3,400rpm |
| Maximum torque | 76Nm at 2,000rpm |
| Fuel consumption (average) | 25 to 30mpg (11–9 litres/100km) |
| Top speed (quoted) | 50mph (80kph) |

## 1954

The Ambulance was fitted with a fuel gauge from 1 April, Volkswagen finally recognising that a reserve gallon and fuel tap was neither appropriate, nor practical. Nevertheless, it would be several more years before the rest of the range were so equipped. Truly a 1 April gesture!

With effect from 31 August, pistons were of the flat crown variety, having previously been trough shaped.

## 1955

As technology advanced and the cost of producing curved glass dropped, the rear quarter windows of the Samba became glass instead of Plexiglas, the change occurring on 18 February.

## The first face-lift for the Transporter

Today, a face-lift is such a common occurrence, invariably happening within two or three years of a model's launch, and usually centring round the cosmetic appearance of the vehicle, that, despite the hype of a press launch, few would-be purchasers take lasting notice. While Nordhoff would have been the last to admit that he was equally rigorous in keeping his range up-to-date, branding stylists as 'hysterical', he was a great advocate of genuine improvements to his range. While gradual evolution was the norm, such tactics weren't always practical. Hence, the Beetle was given a major revamp in October 1952, involving trim, dashboard and technical specification. (Although the car's appearance changed again in March 1953, the replacement of two single panes of glass with one oval-shaped one was hardly earth shattering.)

↓ This unusual angle shot, taken to show the optional equipment opening front windows (M113), also beautifully illustrates the design change made to the Transporter in March 1955, known to most as the 'peaked cap'. The peak was introduced to develop an adequate system of cabin ventilation, the starting point for which was the two grilles visible in this view.

A second significant revamp for the Beetle came in 1957, when a much larger rear window and a second totally new dashboard formed the fulcrum of the transformation. As for the Beetle-based Karmann Ghia 'sports' car, after four years of production, it too saw substantial changes concentrated mainly around the position of the car's headlamps. If Nordhoff had been alive today, he would have undoubtedly argued with some justification that each major change was far from cosmetic and might well have cited the Transporter's overhaul of March 1955 as a classic case of updating its appearance to offer practical solutions to past problems.

By 1955, two major issues had emerged concerning the Transporter's continued success. First, owners were unable to load goods, shopping, or anything else into the rear of the vehicle, the natural 'boot' space in the case of the latter, and the logical point from which to stow lengthy items in the former instance. Secondly, ventilation was poor, despite the fitting of quarter-lights from day one, and well ahead of the Beetle in this respect. The Ambulance's special tailgate had demonstrated that the issues surrounding a rear-opening hatch were not insurmountable, and there

↑ Between March 1955 and August 1963, all Transporters were fitted with 15in wheels and shod with 6.40 x 15 tyres. Note the four narrow slots between the rim and the centre.
↓ With effect from March 1955, the engine compartment lid and petrol filler flap were opened with what enthusiasts term the 'church key', due to its exceptional size.

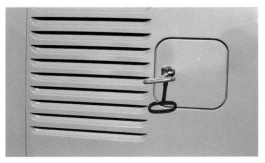

↑ The full-length dashboard was introduced as part of the general modifications to the Transporter's specification in March 1955. Previously, all models but the Microbus Deluxe relied on a single binnacle, while the design of the pre-March 1955 full-length dash on the top-of-the-range model differed from the latest specification.

↓ After a relatively brief period of struggling with antiquated semaphores, American-market Transporters were endowed with flashing front indicators, now known as bullet indicators, in April 1955. European-market models finally received modern flashers in the summer of 1960.

had been an 'M' option that offered a small opening hatch above the barn door, while the official fitting of an accessory air-scoop to the same vehicle and the need for its recognition as an officially sanctioned extra with its own 'M' code confirmed that ventilation issues could also be resolved.

From March 1955 all models, with for obvious reasons the exception of the Pick-up, were fitted with an opening tailgate, similar in size to that offered on the Ambulance, but top rather than bottom piano-style hinged. The tailgate was supported when opened by a stay on its right-hand side. A 'T'-handle was employed to open and close the tailgate. A much smaller engine lid replaced the barn door version. Although the engine compartment was much reduced in size, and the oil-bath air-cleaner had to be moved to the left side as a consequence, servicing the unit remained relatively straightforward as far as access was concerned. To make certain that reduced space didn't equate with the engine getting hotter on longer journeys, the number of vents designed for this purpose was increased from eight to nine, although each was 4mm shorter.

The fuel tank was relocated and sat over the right-hand side of the gearbox, while the resized fuel filler, previously 80mm (3.2in) and now 60mm (2.4in), neck complete with a conventional flap, could be found immediately in front of the engine vents, above the rear wheel-arch. The cap was opened by a key, which thanks to its large size, was christened the 'church key' by enthusiasts, and has remained another god of Splitty mythology as a consequence ever since. The key served a dual purpose, as it was also used to lock the engine compartment lid. The spare wheel, the only other casualty of the tailgate's introduction, was relocated to a position behind the cab bench seat, complete with its own well and noticeable in the bulkhead, mimicking the precedent already set by the Ambulance and the Pick-up. As a consequence of the smaller engine compartment, the load area of the Panel van, or the Kombi when it was devoid of seats, was increased and amounted to 4.8cu metres compared to 4.6cu metres previously.

At the Transporter's front end, the roof panel was revised so that it protruded over the split windowpanes, very much looking as though the Splitty had acquired a peaked cap as worn by schoolboys in the 1950s. While accidentally improving the vehicle's frontal aesthetics, the real purpose was to allow room for an air-scoop to be placed as close as possible to

↑ Until the 1965 model year, all Microbuses had chromed hubcaps with the VW logo highlighted in black, white, or body-colour.

→ The taillights on the first Transporter evolved over the years. This is the final incarnation for European models, which appeared in August 1961. Larger than previous offerings, American-spec taillights of the same vintage looked similar, other than having a red, rather than orange, indicator segment. The vehicle can be identified as a Microbus Deluxe by the trim on the bumper. Note also the American-spec bumpers with large overrider and additional bar.

the top of the vehicle's windscreen, where maximum air turbulence could be found when the vehicle was on the move. Fixed to the cab roof was a connecting air collection and distribution box, which was controllable by a metal handle positioned on its side. Ventilation issues should have been a thing of the past! Concurrent with the peak was a 15mm increase in the height of the split screen panes, while the so-called wing-mirror was relocated to the driver's door hinge.

To complete the external changes of any significance, the diameter of the wheels was decreased by one inch to 15in, while the once-solid centres now sported four narrow cooling slots between the rim and the centre. The tyres fitted to the new wheels were slightly less skinny at 6.40 × 15s, compared with 5.50 × 16s previously. Although the changes were made for eminently practical reasons once more, the overall effect was nevertheless to create a Transporter more in keeping with the times in terms of its appearance.

Inside the Transporter, the most noticeable change was the insertion of a full-length dashboard for all models. Different in appearance to that fitted to the pre-March 1955 Microbus Deluxe and incorporating a kind of metal parcel shelf, the single-instrument VDO speedometer was also home to all the warning lights, while the wiper and headlamp switches were positioned on the left- and right-side of the steering column respectively. A combined starter and ignition switch was attached to the right-hand side of what now passed as an instrument binnacle; while the semaphores were operated from a slim stalk positioned to the left of the steering column.

Sadly, for aficionados of the old three-spoke steering wheel, this was replaced by a more matter-of-fact two-spoke item, although it was still produced in ivory for the more up-market vehicles. As a sign of the times the ashtray remained a prominent feature behind the central spine and between the two split panes of the windscreen. A nice styling touch was the vertical 'vents' in the centre of the dash complete with a protruding and removable off-centre fluted panel. This arrangement was for a radio and speaker if fitted! The passenger grab handle of old was thought to be superfluous now they had a dash to hold on to, while for the driver, what most consider to be an unnecessary change, the original beaver-tail-shaped accelerator was changed for a rectangular and certainly more conventional pedal.

Undoubtedly the face-lift given to the Transporter in March 1955 was the most visually significant in its 17-year production, with some introductions such as the peak and dashboard remaining more-or-less unchanged thereon. However, as the years passed by significant advances in performance occurred, an aspect that was absent from the activities of 1955, while in terms of modifications to keep the Transporter both up-to-date and safe on the road the process was never-ending.

## Year-by-year specification revisions April 1955–July 1967

### 1955
While many manufacturers were readily abandoning antiquated semaphores in favour of modern flashing indicators, Volkswagen stuck rigidly to what was known, at least in Europe. Safety conscious USA (plus Canada and Guam) however, received modern indicators, bullet style, at the front with effect from 1 April 1955.

↓ **Volkswagen's toolkits of the Nordhoff era were substantial affairs containing more than the basics required with one notable exception, those supplied after 1954 lacked the air-cooled engine's all-important spare fan belt. Of note here is the ring for removing hubcaps while the red box containing a spare set of bulbs was an additional purchase the wise often made.**

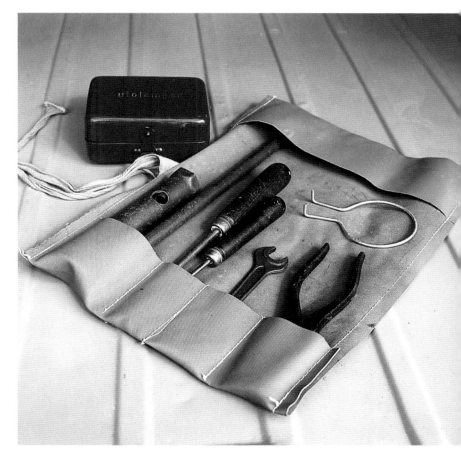

## 1956

The VW logo on the hubcaps previously painted in the body-colour of the Transporter was now, 13 August, always finished in black only.

## 1957

From 5 April, US-spec. Transporters were fitted with combined brake and taillights. The hubcaps on Panel vans and Pick-ups were no longer chromed; instead being painted after 6 August, while in September, indicators became self-cancelling on all models.

## 1958

On 1 May 1958 the single, central brake light was deleted and the engine lid pressing changed accordingly. The brake lights were incorporated into larger taillights at either side of the rear of the vehicle.

The Samba and Microbus Deluxe were fitted with padded vinyl sun-visors from 1 August, replacing the previous fibreboard ones. Finger recesses were added to the reinforced loading door handles on all models. Similarly, stronger cab handles with new recessed lock areas were fitted.

Stronger bumpers with longer blades were

introduced for all non-USA models on 29 August, while on the same day, American-specification models acquired a new style of two-tier bumper with substantial overriders in order that they complied with legislation. The new style proved popular and quickly became an option across European markets.

On 18 December the Pick-up's taillights were positioned 100mm lower and 12mm nearer the sides of the vehicle, while on the 29th of the same month this modification was passed to the rest of the range.

## 1959

With effect from 1 January a hubcap remover device became standard in the toolkit.

In May 1959, the Transporter's engine was replaced with another 30bhp unit! Outwardly distinguishable from its predecessor by its detachable alloy dynamo pedestal, it demonstrated greater efficiency. Bore and stroke remained the same, although the compression ratio was raised a little. The crankcase halves were much stronger, as were the retaining studs and bolts. Cooling was improved, as the cylinder barrels were further apart than previously, while valve diameters were increased. The speed of the cooling fan was reduced, suggesting less engine noise.

From 9 October the engine compartment sealing was improved.

## 1960

The most important event in 1960 occurred on 1 June with the introduction of a further new engine, this time offering 34bhp. The Solex 28PCI carburettor was replaced by the 28PICT, fitted with thermostatically controlled automatic choke and a pre-heated oil bath air cleaner. The ratio of the reduction gears in the axle hubs was changed from 1.4:1 to 1.39:1. The result was livelier performance, despite little if any alteration to the top speed. The key elements were better acceleration through the gears and smoother overall running.

*When the driver's seat became separate to the general bench in the cab, the space for the spare wheel, which sat behind the seats, was increased by enlarging the protrusion into the load compartment. (The fold-down seat is part of the equipment associated with a fire vehicle.)*

| 34BHP ENGINE | |
| --- | --- |
| Capacity | 1,192cc |
| Bore and stroke | 77mm x 64mm |
| Compression ratio | 7.0:1 |
| Maximum power | 34bhp at 3,600rpm |
| Maximum torque | 82Nm at 2,000rpm |
| Fuel consumption (average) | 30mpg |
| | (9 litres/100km) |
| Top speed (quoted) | 50mph (80kph) |

Also with effect from 1 June, the speedometer was re-calibrated to 120kph, (previously 100kph) and no longer featured red gear-change guidance marks. Flashing indicators were fitted to all European market models, finally catching up with the US specification, while the ignition/starter was fitted with a non-repeat lock.

## 1961

The majority of changes took place on 31 July and included new-style and larger two-section rear lights with orange indicator lens (red in the USA), half-moon-shaped shallow recess in the tailgate above the 'T'-handle, column-mounted starter switch, upper corners of the speedometer binnacle more rounded, colour of indicator lights in speedometer housing changed from red to green, and, at long last, a fuel gauge.

American specification models were fitted from 31 July with a larger and much flatter indicator lens, which soon acquired the enthusiast nickname of 'fish-eye'.

## 1962

The most significant changes in the Transporter's specification took place on 30 July. The spare wheel well behind the cab seats was made noticeably deeper, causing a more significant intrusion into the load compartment. The main reason for this change was that the driver's seat was now separate from the passenger bench, although too close for anything to be inserted in the gap in between. Consequently, driver comfort was greatly increased, particularly as the separate seat was adjustable. The wheel arches, both front and rear were enlarged, while a reinforcing lip was added on the rear one.

From 15 October, the word 'Volkswagen' was added centrally above the engine lid. As of 20th November stronger door locks were fitted to all models.

## 1963

The calendar year 1963 proved to be an important one in the history of the first-generation Transporter, as not only did the 1500 engine make its debut, albeit initially only for the US market, but also the look of the Splitty was modernised by a much larger tailgate window, while as Christmas approached, 14in wheels had become standard.

↑ The 1,493cc, 42bhp engine, invariably referred to as the 1500, had a recommended top speed of 65mph (105kph).

→ At the end of July 1961, and just a year after European-market vehicles had acquired bullet indicators, American customers were allocated larger, flatter front indicators that have since been endowed with the enthusiasts' term of 'fish-eye' indicators for rather obvious reasons. European-market Transporters followed suit in August 1963 for the '64 model year.

### 42BHP ENGINE, THE 1500

Available for US models from 7 January 1963, and on selected European models from March.

| | |
|---|---|
| **Capacity** | 1,493cc |
| **Bore and stroke** | 83mm x 69mm |
| **Compression ratio** | 7.5:1 |
| **Maximum power Recommended** | 42bhp at 3,800rpm |
| **Maximum speed** | 65mph (105kph) |
| **Carburettor** | Solex 28PICT |

As a result of the new engine's extra power the payload went up from 750kg (¾ tonne) to 1,000kg (1 tonne), the reduction gear ratio was now 1.26:1. Braking was improved thanks to larger drums.

On 6 March the number of engine cooling vents was increased from nine to ten, while the louvres faced inwards instead of outwards as previously.

After numerous requests, a sliding door option to replace the double loading doors became available on 16 April, (M161).

With effect from 5 August the rear window (in a wider tailgate) (1,230mm x 730mm, 48.4in x 28.7in) became much larger, making reversing manoeuvres much easier. The tailgate's 'T'-handle was replaced

with a push-button style of lock and a finger recess below, while the previous support bracket was replaced with a spring-loaded opening, held in position by what Volkswagen described as 'crossed torsion bars'. A direct consequence of fitting the larger tailgate to the Microbus Deluxe was that there was no longer room for the two windows in the greatly slimmed down rear-quarter panels. European models caught up with the US specification in regard to fitting of fish-eye indicators in place of bullet style. The tail-script badge bearing the word Volkswagen was relocated to the left-hand side of the tailgate.

From 7 November the oil-bath air-cleaner was mounted to the right of the engine, rather than to the left as previously. The cab doors were fitted with push-button style handles on models produced on or after 18 December and by the following day, 14in wheels had become standard, replacing the previous 15in ones.

### 1964

The heating arrangements were amended on 14 April with the installation of a lever-operated flap between the defroster vent and the foot-well vent. The vertical pipe arrangement in the cab was discontinued in favour of two louvred vents. As of 3 August the speed limiter was standard on 1500 Transporters, while larger, more powerful, self-parking wipers were introduced.

The Microbus and Samba benefited from a vinyl headlining (replacing the previous woollen version) as of 30 September. (This style of headlining lining had previously been an 'M' option from 23 April in the previous year.)

### 1965

Although it might be newsworthy that the 1200 engine was finally discontinued as an option for all Transporters in October, the main improvements were more-or-less limited to 2 August and the start of production of 1966 model year vehicles. An upgraded version of the 1500 engine became standard. An extra 2bhp was gained by fitting larger diameter valves (inlet valves 35.5mm, previously 31.5mm, and exhaust valves 32mm, previously 30mm). The engine now developed a maximum of 44bhp at 4,000rpm. The carburettor was a Solex 28PICT-1.

The church key engine lid lock was replaced by a push button with finger grip. Windscreen wipers became two-speed, with a rotary three-speed switch replacing the previous pull-out version.

The headlamp switch became a rotary rubber knob, while the dipswitch was no longer foot operated, being relocated to the steering column. Emergency flashers with a separate switch became standard on export models and the oil filler neck was enlarged.

The Pick-up models benefited from a larger rear cab window, while the previously unaltered eight outward-facing engine cooling vents became three sets of horizontally positioned, inward-facing vents over the rear wheel.

### 1966

While the introduction of the second-generation Transporter was only 12-months away when the '67 model year specification was introduced in August 1966, it didn't prevent Volkswagen from continuing the process of Splitty improvement.

With effect from 2 May, carburettor pre-heating was from the heat exchanger, rather than the cylinder head. On 1 August 12-volt electrics, previously option M620, replaced the much-criticised 6-volt system.

The flywheel was enlarged with 130 teeth instead of the previous 109 and the gearbox case was modified to accept the larger 12-volt starter motor. The tailgate was opened by a new push button with finger grip, while the panel indent of old was deleted. The bumpers had modified pointed ends, replacing the slash style, while dual-circuit braking and reversing lights became standard on some export models, most notably for the US market.

The final first-generation Transporter came off the Hanover assembly line in July 1967, bearing the chassis number 217 148 459.

← From March 1955, first-generation Transporters were endowed with nine engine cooling vents, whereas previously there had been eight. The next change came in March 1963, after which Transporters had ten vents, as seen here.

↓ The eight louvre pattern outward-facing engine-cooling vents on the Pick-up remained in place from the start of production until the end of the 1965 model year, when nine inward-facing vents in three banks of three were introduced, as illustrated.

# CHAPTER 3
# SECOND-GENERATION TRANSPORTER
# THE BAY 1968–1979

With just one instantly noticeable face-lift in its 12-year history, and a full set of options ranging from the Panel van to the equivalent of the first-generation Microbus Deluxe available from launch, only one complication arises in the second-generation Transporter or Bay Window's story and that relates to engines. The Bay started life as a 1600 model and while this survived to the last days of production, the rapid succession of 1700, 1800 and 2000 engines tied to twin carburettors, fuel injection, and even an automatic box, ensures that the Bay's story cannot appear too cursory.

## New model for old

Although Volkswagen's designers had theoretically started with a blank drawing board when considering a replacement for the Splitty, one unwritten rule was sacrosanct. The new model would remain primarily a box on wheels, with an air-cooled engine at the rear, a central cargo area, plus the driver and passengers sat over the front wheels. As such, the basic principles of the first-generation's tried-and-tested construction were maintained. A well-built frame continued to be incorporated into the main body structure; unitary construction had been retained. The chassis frame consisted of two longitudinal members that embraced the entire length of the vehicle, literally from top to tail. These in turn were braced with hefty cross-members and reinforced outriggers to support both the sills and the outer bodywork.

Overall, the new model at 4,420mm (174in) was 140mm (5.5in) longer than the Splitty it replaced at 4,280mm (168.5in). The wheelbase remained the same at 2,400mm, the increase in length being achieved by a greater overhang at both the front and rear. Taken as a whole, the width of the two models was similar, the Bay measuring 1,765mm (69.5in) and the Splitty 1,750mm (68.9in). The same was true of the height of the two models, with the Bay Panel van equating to 1,976mm (77.8in) and the Splitty to 1,925mm (75.8in).

At 5 cubic metres, the usable space in the Bay's interior was greater than that of the Splitty at 4.8 cubic metres, not only due to the increase in length of the vehicle, but also to the comparatively lower floor. That the designer's could arrange this, was in turn a result of incorporating a double-joint rear axle with semi trailing arms, compared to the Splitty's more cumbersome swinging axle system. It shouldn't be a surprise that Volkswagen's independent torsion bar system remained a feature of the new model, primarily thanks to its simple layout and robust nature. The torsion bar tubes were attached as an integral part of the chassis, making for a much stronger and stiffer arrangement.

Although improvements in road holding might be attributed partly to the revised set-up, the main reason was undoubtedly a result of an increase in track, which now stood at 1,426mm (56.1in) at the rear, and 1,384mm (45.5in) at the front.

The Splitty's king and link pin arrangement was cast aside in favour of maintenance-free ball joints, while the fact that reduction gearboxes were a thing of the past helped to increase the sprung and un-sprung weight ratio, improving the ride quality and helping the vehicle to stay more firmly attached to the road in the process.

One area in which the designers were not necessarily as clever was that of overall weight and the consequences thereof. The unladen early second-generation Transporter weighed 1,175kg (2,590lb) according to Volkswagen's publicity. The equivalent late first-generation model had a quoted unladen weight of 1,070kg (2,359lb), making it lighter by 105kg. At a time when Volkswagen's products in general were thought to be somewhat underpowered compared with those of other manufacturers, a weight penalty was the last thing required. Fortunately, the new model benefited from a more powerful engine.

← The second-generation Transporter, nicknamed the Bay due to its panoramic windscreen, was produced from August 1967 to the end of July 1979. Nearly 2.5 million examples were manufactured and at its peak over 250,000 Transporters of all types were built annually. This early example of a Microbus has been converted into a Devon Camper. The Microbus was one of the most popular Transporter options.

## The 1600 engine

Any temptation to really boost the performance of the new model when compared to that of the old was firmly resisted when the second-generation Transporter was launched. With Nordhoff firmly in control throughout the years of the Bay's evolution from design drawing to launch, few would have thought it could be any other way. The 1600 engine that made its debut with the Bay was unquestionably more powerful than the final power plant endowed to the Splitty. But the difference wasn't significant enough for would-be purchasers not to call for more power within a relatively short period and particularly so in the United States.

### 1600 ENGINE

| | |
|---|---|
| Capacity | 1,584cc |
| Bore and stroke | 85.5mm x 69.0mm |
| Compression ratio | 7.7:1 |
| Maximum power | 47bhp at 4,000rpm |
| Maximum torque | 103Nm at 2,200rpm |
| Top and cruising speed | 65mph (105kph) |
| Fuel consumption (average) | 23mpg* |

*Source, US market promotional material (12 litres/100km)

With an American copywriter referring to the new 1600 engine as being 'stronger' and possessing 'a little more horsepower and a lot more torque', literature produced for the British market was equally exuberant.

'The powerful, elastic 1.6-litre engine ... gives you all the power you want. More acceleration. Safer overtaking. It makes the VW Commercial fast and lively. (Its top speed and its cruising speed are one and the same – thanks to air-cooling and low maximum revs.) And it's sturdy, robust and economical – like all VW engines.'

It is also worth noting that the new 1600 was a single-port engine in the best tradition of the 1500 that powered the Splitty in its final years. Twin-port engines were on the horizon however.

## A brand-new body

The brochure designed to mark the launch of the second-generation Transporter in Britain helps to highlight exactly why the Bay was a brand-new model, rather than a revamp of the Splitty. The following extract is taken from the introductory page.

'With its new body it's larger, more elegant. But

at the same time much more practical, too. The full-width, curved windscreen and (in the Kombi and the Clipper) the large side windows mean good visibility and plenty of light inside. The two-speed windscreen wipers have large blades. Generous exterior mirrors project on each side giving a really wide view. Below the windscreen you can see the air intake for the fresh air ventilation system. The flashing indicators up front are new. But this isn't just for art's sake. They're larger, too. Which makes them even easier to see than before. The sturdy wrap-around bumpers are just the right height above the ground – and the front one incorporates a step on either side. No more clambering into the cab. The new VW Commercial is a distinctive, elegant vehicle ...'

Despite the fact that the new single glass windscreen was only 27 per cent larger than the combined total of the two panes in the Splitty, it was this feature more than any other that identified the second-generation Transporter as a new model. Even the vehicle's nickname, the Bay, was a direct reference to the panoramic nature of the screen when compared to that of the Splitty. The other significant change at the front was the grille below the screen

that formed an essential part of the vehicle's fresh-air ventilation system, while adding character to what might otherwise have been deemed to be a rather bland, though at least partially double-skinned, front panel. After all, gone was the 'V'-shaped swage line, which at least as far as some of the Splitty Microbuses went denoted two distinct sections of colour, one above and one below the line, while, in the case of the Samba of old, prominent bright work had highlighted the divide. Now the Clipper L's two-tone paintwork was restricted to the roof panel only, while at the vehicle's front its only distinguishing marks were a

↑ The single-port 1600 engine as fitted to early Bays produced a maximum of 47bhp at 4,000rpm, an improvement over its 1500 predecessor. It was still considerably slower than most American rivals, however.

← The push-button engine lid lock was introduced in August 1965 when the Splitty engine lid was reduced in size. The push button continued throughout the era of the Bay. For the first few years it was chromed as seen here. However, during the hard times of the mid-1970s, cost-cutting measures resulted in the body of the push button being reduced to painted black metal.

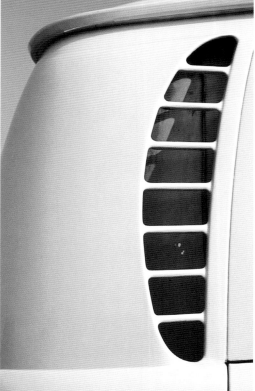

↑ The Kombi in Bay guise was a simplistic affair compared with its more up-market brothers but, as ever, it was a highly versatile vehicle and outsold all other individual models throughout the production run of the second-generation Transporter.

→ The engine cooling vents on early second-generation Transporters were mounted high on the rear quarters, and were both unobtrusive and aesthetically attractive.

discreet trim around the ventilation grille, a bright work insert for the screen rubber and an old faithful, namely a chromed VW roundel on the front.

For the rest of the range, not only was there no chrome, but also once-painted metal was replaced by plastic! Apart from the indicators referred to in the brochure extract above, the front bumper, also mentioned, is worthy of comment. Although within a few years the new Bay bumper would be phased out in favour of a less aesthetically pleasing, but rigidly functional design, its sturdy nature linked as before to a step-up undoubtedly helped the Bay retain some of the character of its predecessor.

Looking at the Bay from the side, four improvements were immediately apparent dependent on the model involved. For a start, all Bays had wind-down cab windows, dispensing with the antiquated sliding panes offered previously. In an age when quarter-lights were still prevalent, most Bay Transporters had fixed panes, but opening windows were usually fitted to the Microbuses, and even to the Kombi. Gone were the side loading doors, changed for the previous extra-cost option of a sliding door. More generously sized cab doors made access far easier for even the stoutest of owners. Finally, where side windows were part of the specification, the shape had changed dramatically. Now two, rather than three, fully rectangular panes filled the vast majority of the upper panels, making the interior appear roomier and definitely lighter. Once totally acceptable, the small, nearly square panes characteristic of the Splitty were clearly no longer in vogue. Sadly, there was one casualty in the modernisation process. Whereas the Samba had stood out from the crowd with its four nearly square panes, the Clipper L, or Microbus L, could only really be spotted by its bright work inserts in the rubber of the window surrounds and a thin trim strip running around the flanks. Although possibly more relevant to the interior description, both the Clipper and Clipper L benefited from opening quarter-lights in the side windows, one located in the sliding door, the other in the rearmost window on the opposite side of the vehicle.

To the rear of the side panels the engine cooling vents were very different from those incorporated into the Splitty's lower panels. Although mounted high, at launch they were relatively unobtrusive, possibly even adding a little character to the somewhat bland side panels of the new model. As an aside, the Pick-up retained the engine air vent arrangement as found on late first-generation models.

To be bluntly honest, a glance at the rear of a late-model Splitty and an early model Bay would leave most casual observers unaware that they were looking at two different generations of vehicle, even though no panel was interchangeable between the two.

While once more only really affecting the Clipper L, the distinctive fold-back sunroof that had always been part of the Samba's composition, became a thing of the past, replaced by a much smaller wind-back steel sunroof, although this was still produced by Golde. With effect from April 1968, the sliding roof could be specified on all models with a sufficiently large roof panel to site one.

Finally, the new version of the High-Roof Panel van utilised glass-fibre rather than metal to form the area that gave the model its name. Although the material was a relatively new invention, and had previously been more or less confined to usage by manufacturers of kit cars as far as the automobile industry was concerned, it had one great advantage over that of metal. While rust was a thing of the past, this paled into insignificance when compared with the issue of weight, or rather the lack of it.

↓ The second-generation Microbus Deluxe was originally known as the Clipper L, but for legal reasons it wasn't long before the first-generation terminology was restored. As this Volkswagen publicity shot illustrates, the top-of-the-range model usually featured two-tone paint, the roof panel to the rain guttering being white. Bright work surrounded each window, and could be found on the swage line below the windows, as well as around the air intake grille at the front of the vehicle. A chrome VW roundel and extra trim on the bumper, together with chrome hubcaps more or less completed the upmarket package.

→ The second-generation High-Roof Panel van differed from its predecessor in that it had a glass-fibre roof panel, rather than a metal one. This weight-saving device was bonded to the top of the bodywork. The example illustrated has been employed for its entire life as an ice-cream vending vehicle, spending many years in Italy before its arrival in Britain.

↓ Microbus versions of the second-generation Transporter benefited from heating in the rear passenger compartment, an extra-cost option on the Kombi. Warm air was ducted along the door trim, linking to tubes at either side, the one in the cab area being just visible. Two-tone panelling on the door card and the padded armrest on the ducting indicate that this is the top-of-the-range Microbus Deluxe.

## Interior design

When it came to the second-generation's interior, and excluding the airy and light look created by the much larger side windows already referred to, two features transformed the look Volkswagen's customers had been used to. Otherwise rubber floor covering, vinyl seating, plus hardboard panelling and a lack of anything more than a basic plastic headlining for the workaday models, was standard.

First, while a walk-through option had been available on first-generation models for many years, it had always been at extra cost. Now, in standard form, all models came with two separate seats in the cab. The driver's seat could be moved both fore and aft offering to its occupant a total of nine different positions, while the backrest was adjustable to any position. Inevitably, some options, most notably the Pick-ups and the Panel van with a complete division between cab and load area, had little need for a gap between the driver's and passenger's seat and in such instances, the latter was a two-seater bench. Likewise, Microbuses could be specified as nine-seater models where transportation of maximum numbers on a regular basis was required.

The second-generation Transporter's dashboard was the other item that transformed both the look and the feel of the vehicle's interior when compared to that of the Splitty. Although the design of the two-spoke steering wheel was new, as this was rather functionally mundane in its appearance, it has to be irrelevant to any praise heaped on the Bay's interior. So cleverly designed was the dashboard that it more or less survived the vehicle's 12-year production run intact. The writers of Volkswagen's Bay literature were justifiably proud of the design team's achievement and the text produced proves more than an adequate lead-in.

'It would grace a passenger car. Everything's there. And just where you want it. From ashtray to parking light tell-tale. The works. The instruments can all be read at a glance. They're well laid out. And non-reflecting. The control knobs are marked with symbols and are so arranged that they can't possibly be confused. The upper edge of the panel is padded black to prevent screen reflection. And for safety. Next to the fresh air vent on the left-hand side of the panel you can see the fuel gauge – complete with tell-tales for generator, high beam, parking lights, oil pressure and turn signals. Next to it is the speedometer. The safety-type ashtray (designed for smokers – by a smoker) falls out of its bracket in the event of a collision. The generous glove compartment will take more than just the odd map, or piece of paper. The grab handle just above it is of flexible material. On the extreme right is a second fresh air vent. Passenger car comfort for driver and front seat passenger ...'

One issue relating to the dashboard does require clarification. All US-bound models were fitted with a fully padded dash, a legislative requirement that had come into effect in the early months of 1967. Elsewhere, painted metal, other than the upper edge of the dash as referred to in the text above, remained standard although a padded version (M511) could be specified at extra cost. Likewise, in what has to be seen as a pointless exercise in penny-pinching, not all models for all markets were provided with a lid for the glovebox.

## Early year specification revisions August 1967–July 1972

### 1967
Very early models were fitted with a 30 PICT-1 carburettor, but with effect from September 1967 this became a 30 PICT-2.

### 1968
In April, the metal sunroof that was part of the standard specification of the Clipper L model became available as an option on other models, (M560).

↓ **The second-generation dashboard was a big improvement on that of the Splitty. Volkswagen brochures of the day proclaimed that 'the new VW Commercial has a new instrument panel to give you genuine finger-tip control'. Big claims were made regarding safety too, 'by including a new safety-type dished steering wheel' and a 'non-reflecting instrument panel padding'.**

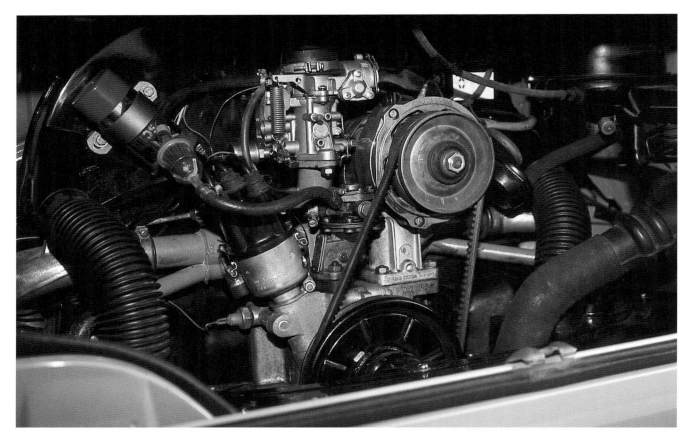

The 1600 twin-port engine, introduced in August 1970, saw the cylinder head modified to give it two inlet ports instead of the previous one. This allowed the engine to breathe more efficiently, increasing maximum power from 47bhp to 50bhp.

→ The 1,700cc engine pictured was the first of the suitcase engines, borrowed from the Type 4 series, to be installed in the Transporter.

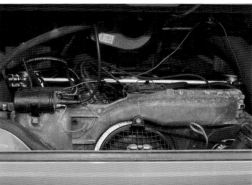

To coincide with the start of production of '69 models in August 1968, the design of the cab door handles was changed to a trigger action rather than the previous press button. The torsion bars on the workaday models, including the Kombi without rear seats, became more robust.

### 1969

All the most important changes made during the year occurred in August and related to the start of '70 model year production. For added protection in the case of an accident, two diagonal beams were added under the cab floor to strengthen it. Similarly, the inner doorframes were strengthened and the steering column became collapsible. Where a padded dash wasn't fitted the metalwork was painted black rather than in the body colour of the vehicle as previously.

Contact switches operating the courtesy light(s) were fitted to the doors. Side-mounted direction indicators and reversing lights were fitted as standard for some markets while side reflectors were changed from round to square on US models. Chrome wheel trims, previously standard on the Microbus L, were no longer fitted.

### 1970

The main changes made during the year all related to the start of '71 model production in August. The cylinder heads of the 1600 engine were modified giving them two inlet ports instead of one and allowing the engine to breathe more easily. Maximum brake horse-power increased from 47 to 50bhp at 4,000rpm. The steel oil cooler was changed for an aluminium one with the purpose of dissipating heat more efficiently. The size of the fan was increased and the inlet manifold modified.

Front ATE disc brakes were introduced replacing hydraulically operated drums. The Transporter continued with five stud wheels throughout the production run of the second-generation model. However, at the same time that disc brakes were introduced the wheel mounting holes were changed, now becoming closer together. The wheels were also mounted with nuts rather than the bolts of earlier days. The style of the wheel itself was also revised in August 1970. Previously 5J × 14in, the wheel modification involved an increase in size to 5½J × 14in and the introduction of a series of round ventilation holes in the outer part of each wheel's centre section, replacing the narrow slots between the rim and centre. The new style of wheel also heralded the demise of the domed hubcap in favour of ones similar in nature to those fitted to the Beetle for a time at this stage. As previously, all models except the Microbus had hubcaps painted in grey, where chrome remained the option. The new wheels were sprayed in silver, having previously been painted white. The design of the rear drum brakes was changed to accommodate the new wheels, while a brake pressure regulator was fitted to help equalise the

pressure between the front and rear under heavy braking pressure.

The appearance of the rear wheel arches was amended to suit the size of the new wheels.

### 1971

The Transporter underwent a further series of improvements at the start of the new model year in August 1971. Most important of all was the introduction of a larger, but initially optional engine, the 1700, to run alongside the 1600 twin-port. (The progression from 1700 to 1800 and 2-litre engines is covered separately below.)

The engine cooling vents (positioned high on the rear quarters) were enlarged, becoming squarer in shape, more prominent and consequently more obtrusive. The change was necessary to suit the larger 1700 engine. Similarly, the engine tin-ware was reshaped to improve cooling. The valance immediately below the engine lid was welded into place, having previously been removable. The engine compartment lid became smaller and the shape of the metal was changed above the number plate.

The fuel filler cap was moved 400mm (15¾in) further back on the body of the vehicle, so that it

←← **With effect from August 1971, the Transporter's taillights became much larger and included a section for reversing lamps. As the Transporter's bumpers were still the rounded style (as fitted to the launch models) and would be for another year, this is an easy way of identifying a 1972 model year Transporter.**

← **In this picture, the later-style taillights are shown together with the box section bumpers fitted on 1973 model year and later Transporters. The reflector is American specification.**

Volkswagen sales training document, ensured that 'without opening a window it is possible to change the air at a rate of 3.6 cubic meters per minute.' Inevitably, the 'swivel' quarter-lights were no longer available as standard, but for those sceptics who preferred not to rely on modern innovations, they could still be specified as an 'M' option.

## The face-lifted Bay Transporter

Although many changes had been made to the second-generation Transporter since its launch in the summer of 1967, come August 1972 for the start of the '73 model year, the Bay underwent a relatively minor visual face-lift that was sufficient for even those with little more than a passing interest in the Transporter to determine whether they were looking at a pre or post-August 1972 model. Behind the Bay's new look there were many other improvements and Volkswagen dealers in Britain were provided with preview details of the key 'advances' as an attachment to the latest brochure.

'The new styling of the front of the Type II range gives a much neater overall appearance, the small side step now being positioned inside the vehicle.

could be filled with the sliding door in the open position (LHD and twin-sliding-door models).

New and much larger taillight clusters were introduced, incorporating clear lower section lenses for reversing lights (where fitted). Previously, the Bay window model had used the same basic elliptical tail lamp arrangement as those fitted to later first-generation models. Where reversing lights had been fitted as an optional extra, or in the USA, the rectangular lamps had been positioned above and separate from the main light cluster.

Finally, the cab doors were fitted with 'adjustable air extractor louvers', which, according to a

'The indicators have been repositioned adding to safety as they are now located in a much more prominent position.

'Besides enhancing appearance, driver and passenger safety has been increased by fitting new bumpers at the front and rear at the recommended international height. They have a new deformation element which brings substantial improvement to the passive safety. Behind the front bumper there is an energy-absorbing box profile which together with the frame reinforcement in the doors, form an effective front-end crumple zone. The warm air and ventilation controls have been simplified, they are as follows: Instead of four levers there are now only three. The left lever (red knob) controls all heating air flaps, the middle lever (red knob) controls the hot air flow while the right lever (blue knob) controls the ventilation flow [on RHD vehicles this order is reversed].

'The switch for the windscreen wipers is now on the steering column. This is more convenient. It also has an additional fitting for the slow wiper process. As an added safety feature these controls are easier to operate when wearing safety belts.

'The improvement in the thickness of the brake lining for the disc brakes by almost 50 per cent naturally means longer life and added safety. The exhaust systems have been nickel-plated which will make them last longer because they are better protected against corrosion.

'The intake air pre-heating has been improved on the 1.6 litre models, the pre-heating phase has been lengthened and the accelerator pump now works with a thermostatic control. The new worm roll steering gives more positive control in all conditions.

'Finally, the most significant modification to the Type II model range this model year will be the introduction of the automatic transmission on the 1700 models. This will fill a vital gap with commercial users especially in towns and cities. Not many other manufacturers offer automatics with commercials and few can approach the VW automatic in terms of quality, reliability and price.'

Offering a little more correlative detail, the visual changes consisted of the following. The prominent VW roundel was substantially reduced in size and positioned lower on the nose panel. The front indicators, previously positioned close to the bumper

↓ **This later-model Double Cab Pick-up inevitably features square-section bumpers amongst the other characteristics of vehicles of this vintage. Rarely seen however are the black 'over-riders', in reality optional-equipment (M288) headlight washers.**

were repositioned at either end of the fresh air inlet grille. Previously slim and rectangular, the new indicators were both larger and squarer. The main purpose in moving the indicators was to make them more visible to oncoming vehicles. The bright trim around the fresh air inlet grille on the Microbus Deluxe was no longer fitted. Stronger, energy-absorbing, square-shaped bumpers, similar in profile to those fitted to 1300 and 1500, 1302S and 1303 Beetles built after August 1967, replaced the rounded outline version previously fitted. As a consequence, the cab step, which had been an integral part of the original wraparound bumper was positioned inside the cab, making the vehicle

look more modern but also rather austere.

At the rear, the new model year Transporter was little changed, but the new bumper had the effect of making what had happened look very different. The Volkswagen script attached to the tailgate was deleted and the revamped engine lid of a year ago was further modified, with the bulge housing the number-plate light becoming more prominent.

A glance at the side of the vehicle would have revealed a revision to the sliding door's handle, involving a separate rather than integral lock and a much smaller recess in the panel as the handle no longer moved as far to open the door.

Improvements, or additions, to the '73 model specification that weren't visually obvious included: Recessed piston crowns for the 1600 engine; worm-and-peg steering replaced by worm-and-roller; hot air vents under the windscreen changed to start the demisting process in the middle rather than the lower part of the screen; heater and air distribution controls changed simplifying the operation for owners; brake fluid reservoir relocated from its previous position under the dashboard to a site under the driver's seat; the design of both front disc brakes and associated callipers changed, becoming wider while stub axles lengthened; seat backrests designed to be fitted

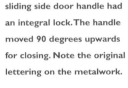 Until August 1972, the sliding side door handle had an integral lock. The handle moved 90 degrees upwards for closing. Note the original lettering on the metalwork.

↓ The later style of door handle had a separate lock and required less movement to open it.

with detachable headrests (previously optional extra integral headrest) – an extra-cost option for all Microbuses; battery repositioned to make access to terminals easier, and the cab floor redesigned to incorporate crumple zone.

Although neither visually obvious, nor particularly convenient for campers and owners storing goods on the rear-loading shelf, due to the flatter design of the 1700 engine an inspection hatch was fitted into the panel above the engine and accessed through the tailgate. This removable hatch afforded easier entry for any type of work undertaken on the suitcase-style engine, and realistically should have been part of the previous year's upgrade and thus coinciding with the arrival of the new shape of engine.

With the sole exception of the Pick-up all Transporters with a 1700 engine were now available with a three-speed automatic gearbox. In Britain at least the 'automatic transmission with hydrodynamic torque converter' option was only available to special order.

## 1700, 1800 and 2-litre engines

Discounting the gain in brake horse-power brought about by the introduction of the 1600 in twin-port guise, the first of Volkswagen's stock of engines to be offered in the Transporter that presented more power for would-be purchasers was the 1700. This made its debut in August 1971, at the start of the '72 model year. As an aside, it is worth noting that potential purchasers of Italian-market Transporters should be aware that with effect from January 1971 it was possible for would-be owners to specify a 1300 engine. For most today this unit would be too underpowered to be effective in a vehicle of the Transporter's size and weight.

The 1700 engine was not intended to replace the 1600, at least as far as the European market was concerned, but to run alongside it as a more powerful option, complete with 'M' code. Indeed, at least initially, the Pick-up was not available in 1700 guise. However, American and Canadian-bound Transporters proved to be the exception to the rule as all body options, including the Pick-up and its derivatives, were fitted with the 1700 from the first day that it was available.

The choice of words above relating to the 1700 is significant, for this engine wasn't purpose-built for

the Transporter, as it had already seen service in the largest of the air-cooled saloon/variant range, the 411. In that vehicle it was housed under what might best be described as a glorified parcel shelf in the saloon and under the loading area to the rear of the car in the variant. Like the VW 1500/1600, or Type 3, before and concurrent with the 411, such a design of bodywork didn't lend itself to the upright stance of the traditional Beetle or Transporter engines. Enthusiasts quickly came to name the compact and much flatter power plants required for these vehicles as 'suitcase' engines. To achieve this goal, the cooling fan was located on the end of the much-stronger crankshaft at the rear of the engine. The fan in turn was enclosed within an aluminium-alloy housing designed to conduct air over the engine in a funnelled arrangement of ducts.

Apart from satisfying the requirements of bodywork design in the Type 3 and Type 4 series, most would acknowledge that such a system permitted more efficient cooling. On the plus side of the layout of a suitcase engine, at least in the Transporter, the Bosch coil, dynamo and oil filter

↑ With effect from August 1971 the size of the cooling vents was increased, and they were reworked to stand proud from the side of the vehicle. The changes were made to accommodate cooling the new and larger 1,700cc engine.

printed for the British and selected European markets referred to SAE rather than bhp. The following is Volkswagen's own specification for the 1700 engine.

'Air-cooled, four-cylinder, four-stroke flat-four engine mounted in the rear. Capacity 1,679cc. Output: SAE 74bhp at 5,000rpm. Compression ratio 7.3 to 1. Maximum torque 85.3ft lb at 3,400rpm (SAE). Twin down-draught carburettors with automatic choke. Thermostatically controlled fan air-cooling. Oil cooler ... Differences on models with automatic transmission SAE 70bhp at 4,200rpm, Max. torque 87ft lb at 3,200rpm (SAE)'

Using Volkswagen's quoted performance figures, the 1700 was capable of a top speed of 78mph (125kph) and averaged 22mpg (13 litres/100km), which compared to a top speed of 68mph (109kph) with the 1600 and a slightly more economical fuel consumption figure of 24.8mpg (11.4 litres/100km). Perhaps not entirely a surprise there was no reference to 0–60mph (0–96.5kph) performance in Wolfsburg's literature. However, contemporary road tests suggested reasonably respectable figures of between 22.3 and 24 seconds and a quarter mile performance of 21.4 seconds, a full eight seconds better than that of the 1600. On the downside, one of the same reports recorded a dismal 18.3mpg (15.5 litres/100km) as an overall figure for petrol consumption. Consolation came in the form of an even more dismal record for the 1600 set back in 1968 by the same magazine, when fuel economy stood at a mere 17.3mpg (16.4 litres/100km).

Bearing in mind that the face-lifted VW 411, designated the 412 when it was launched in August 1972, was endowed with an 1800 engine from the start of the '74 model year, it won't come as a great surprise to discover that the 1700's partnership with the Transporter was relatively short-lived. In November 1973, the 1700 was dropped in favour of the 1,795cc, 68bhp engine. The new engine was to the same basic design as that of 1700, the capacity increase being achieved by enlarging the bore from 90mm to 93mm. Larger diameter inlet and outlet valves, 39.3mm to 41mm and 33.0mm to 34mm respectively, only resulted in a apparently disappointing increase of 2bhp over the 66bhp of the 1700. The equally negligible increase in top speed was neither here nor there, but the boost in torque from 81lb ft at 3,200rpm to 92.4lb ft at 3,000rpm was more than worthwhile.

**↑ As a result of constant demands for more power than the 1600 engine could offer in the second-generation Transporter, the decision was taken to utilise the suitcase-style 1,679cc engine developed for Volkswagen's largest and most recently introduced passenger vehicle, the now relatively unknown VW 411.**

neck all sat lower in the engine bay and were easily accessible. Conversely, access to the carburettors, spark plugs and distributor was nowhere near as good as it had been and would remain with the upright 1600 and its Splitty predecessors. To alleviate such difficulties a partial solution was the introduction of a hatch fitted in the Transporter's rear luggage bay directly above the engine, an 'improvement' already noted in the summary of year-by-year changes listed above.

Students of the VW 411 will be aware that at launch its 1700 engine was fitted with twin carburettors, although after a relatively short period fuel injection had been introduced in an attempt to boost sluggish sales. In Nordhoff's time, the idea of the Transporter being offered with anything other than a single Solex was unthinkable, but the spirit of Volkswagen had changed. Perhaps fuel injection would have been too radical, but twin carburettors were fitted in the form of two Solex 34 PDSITs, sat over short-travel manifolds. Not only was the perennial problem of icing up in cold weather solved, but also the boost in power over and above that of the 1600 was significant; 50bhp with the 1600, 66bhp with the 1700.

Bore and stroke stood at 90mm x 60mm with the 1,679cc engine and the maximum of 66bhp was developed at 4,800rpm. Curiously even material

The majority of owners appear to have achieved around 26mpg (11 litres/100km), a saving of a little over one-mile per gallon. Other modifications relating to the arrival of the 1800 engine included making the cylinder walls thicker, as a straightforward boring out of the 1700 would have left them worryingly thin. While the inlet ports were slightly amended in shape the clutch springs were strengthened and the traditional oil-bath air-cleaner was replaced by one with a paper element.

Restrictive regulations sweeping across America, and of a particularly swingeing nature in California, meant that the supply of the suitcase engine with twin carburettors there was no longer acceptable. In March 1974, a fuel-injected version of the 1800 engine became standard for that state, while in August of the same year the rest of America and the whole of Canada followed suit. The fuel injection system by Bosch was airflow controlled, (AFC) and comprised an electrically controlled computer unit and sensors; fuel injectors, plus fuel lines and

induction manifolds. Unlike some others, this was not a direct injection system, and the fuel injectors sprayed fuel into the induction housings. The amount of fuel injected was both dependent on the amount of incoming air and the engine revolutions. Although complex, the fuel-injected engine tended to be reliable.

The final engine in the sequence of upgrades was the 2-litre offering. With the demise of the 412 in July 1974, at least in saloon form, to make way for the new water-cooled Passat, Volkswagen had to look elsewhere in the range for its new Transporter engine. Fortunately the mid-engine, joint project, VW Porsche 914 sports car, originally introduced in 1969, provided the solution. The 914 had benefited from a 2-litre engine since the start of the '73 model year. As far as the Transporter was concerned, the first vehicles to be fitted with the 2-litre engine were those released in August 1975 as part of the '76 model year revisions.

Not only was the bore increased again, this time to 94mm, but also the stroke was lifted to 71mm

↓ **This late-model Microbus Deluxe differs from the launch model of August 1967. For the 1968 to 1970 model years two-tone paint changed colour at the roof gutter. From the 1971 model year, the change was under the belt line. While bright work still abounded on post-August 1972 models, it was no longer included around the air intake grille, while the side trim moved from the belt line to run in line with the door handles. The sliding sunroof introduced in April 1968 as part of the Microbus Deluxe package was deleted in August 1973, becoming an extra-cost option.**

↑ This Brazilian-built
Microbus features a Bay
front end and Split-screen
bodywork to the rear of
the cab. Late Bay rear
lights look very much like
an afterthought.

from its previous 60mm. However, this was the extent of the changes on this occasion, as even the valve sizes of the 1800 were retained. The result was an engine with an output of 70bhp at 4,200rpm. Ever conservative, Volkswagen declared in its British market literature a top speed for the new engine of 79mph (76mph with automatic transmission), although Volkswagen of America was even more negative with its desultory 75mph.

In reality, once the 2-litre engine was suitably bedded in, it was not unknown for Transporters to reach 100mph and not only when travelling downhill! An eight per cent increase in torque, 143Nm (105lb ft) at 2,800rpm, ensured even greater hill-climbing ability than the 1800 and left owners of the 1600 engine Transporter standing, literally. Volkswagen claimed overall fuel consumption for the 2-litre to be 22.6mpg with a manual gearbox, or 21.2mpg in three-speed automatic guise. As a comparison, the same document indicated 24.8mpg for the 1600, while Volkswagen of America's 1977 brochure gave a 'highway' figure for the 2-litre of 26mpg and an alarming 'city' reading of just 16mpg.

## Latter year specification revisions August 1973–July 1979

Having previously referred to calendar years and noted that the vast majority of modifications and improvements related to the new model year, for the remaining period of Bay production model years are indicated with calendar dates shown in brackets. Few will fail to notice that as the end of production approached improvements made to the outgoing model were strictly limited.

### '74 MODEL YEAR (AUGUST 1973)

In what appeared to be a cost-cutting exercise, the fuel filler flap and attendant recess for the cap were deleted, leaving the latter flush with the surrounding bodywork.

The sliding sunroof was no longer a standard part of the Microbus Deluxe's specification.

The headlamp rims were of a different design necessitating their removal to adjust the headlamps.

Minor changes to dashboard instruments and controls, plus rougher paint surface where padding was not part of the specification.

### '75 MODEL YEAR (AUGUST 1974)

Another albeit in-vogue cost-cutting measure occurred when both the engine lid and rear-hatch handles were changed from chromed metal to black plastic. Similarly, the stainless steel external rear view mirror cases were replaced by ones of painted steel on all but the Deluxe models.

The interior light in the rear compartment was no longer controlled from the dashboard.

### '76 MODEL YEAR (AUGUST 1975)

The bolts to mount engine to gearbox became longer. The Pick-up was now available with an automatic gearbox linked to a 2-litre engine (not 1600).

### '77 AND '78 MODEL YEARS (AUGUST 1976 AND AUGUST 1977)

August 1977 – the steering wheel was redesigned with a thicker rim and spokes. A sliding side window was added to the sliding door on Kombi and Microbus models, plus the Ambulance.

### '79 MODEL YEAR

A catalyst converter was fitted on all USA or Canadian-bound Transporters (only the 2-litre engine was available).

## And finally

Although production of the second-generation Transporter wasn't due to finish until the last day of July 1979, production of its successor, the T3, started in May.

For those with an avid interest in dating a second-generation Transporter by changes in its visual appearance, as a postscript to the main improvements or changes made over the production run, here are two helpful paint or trim related tips, both of which are most closely related to the progress of the Microbus Deluxe. Where the upper panels of a Bay were painted in a different shade to those of the lower ones, between 1968 and 1970, the join came in the rain gutter, whereas after that date it came immediately under the raised waistline. Until the end of July 1974 the Microbus was adorned with alloy mouldings along this waistline. For the 1975 model year and after, the design of the strips changed to include a rubber insert and they were positioned a few inches under the waistline. Not many Microbuses bearing this position of trim are seen today, but if one is spotted its alloy mouldings tend to look like a homemade afterthought.

↓ **The Bay version of the Transporter survived in Mexico and Brazil for many years after German production had ceased. The vehicle here is a Mexican example from the 1990s, complete with water-cooled engine, hence the rather ugly radiator appendage with small VW badge.**

# CHAPTER 4
# THIRD-GENERATION TRANSPORTER
# THE WEDGE 1979–1990

Unlike its predecessors, the third-generation Transporter, known officially as the T3 across Europe, the T25 in oddball Britain, the Vanagon in North America, and latterly nicknamed the Wedge in enthusiast circles, was out of step with the rest of Volkswagen's range in 1979. For here was a new flat-four air-cooled model, with its engine at the rear, while all such other vehicles had been ousted from Wolfsburg and its German satellites in favour of the Golf, Polo, Passat, and Scirocco. However, just a few short years into production steps were taken to rectify such a transgression, as first a water-cooled diesel engine purloined from the Golf and then in 1983, special boxer engines, again cooled by water, cast aside old technology for ever. While increasingly luxurious trims linked to a new encyclopaedia of names and model designations, plus a dabble with permanent four-wheel drive in the shape of the syncro, are important aspects of a third-generation chronology, the crux of the Wedge story will always remain the bumpy transition from air to water.

## Model revisions

Like the second-generation model it replaced, all variations on the general Transporter theme were available from the Wedge's launch. Like the Bay too, an element of badge engineering took place, although in this instance there was no inadvertent attempt to borrow names in use by major businesses across the world. Describing the exercise as a 'new feature' alongside genuine enhancements to the Transporter's performance or appearance, Volkswagen proudly proclaimed that 'goods vehicles are badged "Transporter" and personnel carriers are badged "Bus".'

Not all variations were available to all markets, as demonstrated by reference to an early listing of the range on offer in the UK. Under the Transporter heading, apart from the Panel van, High-Roof

Delivery van, and Pick-up, there were two variations of Double Cab Pick-up, one with rear seats and rear side windows and the other without either feature. Additionally, there was the Extended Platform Pick-up. This option, like all the rest was available with a choice of two air-cooled engines.

Under the Bus heading, UK buyers could select between eight- and nine-seat models and specify either standard, or what was described in the accompanying brochure as 'the luxurious Bus L'. Missing from the list was what in the past would have been described as the Kombi, plus seven-seat variations on the Bus theme.

## Comparing new with old

Like its predecessor, the third-generation Transporter was of unitary construction, the body-shell being welded directly on to a chassis frame comprised of two parallel longitudinal box-sections, assisted and strengthened by cross-members and outriggers. Essentially, the majority of the body panels were single skinned but bonded to what amounted to an inner framework. Where additional rigidity was required, as with the cab floor, the main loading or passenger compartment, and the additional luggage/parcel area over the engine, the metalwork was corrugated.

Having established its basic nature, the first things that need noting about the Wedge undoubtedly relate to size and appearance. Put succinctly, the T3 looked noticeably bigger than its predecessor, which it most certainly was, and lacked the rounded, friendly appearance of both the Bay and the Splitty, becoming in the process more akin to the offerings of other manufacturers as a slab-sided, squared-off wedge, or worse still, brick. In a not entirely successful move to counteract the worst excesses of what was a potentially dull appearance, a bold swage line was added at the vehicle's waist, while a second and far less pronounced one cut across the upper elements

← **Although the numbers of the third-generation Transporter manufactured were not as great as those of the Bay, due to the increasing popularity of cheaper Japanese imports, the Wedge was a more practical vehicle than either of its predecessors. Initially retaining either a 1.6- or 2.0-litre air-cooled engine, first a diesel and then water-cooled engines took over. Camper conversions were more luxurious partly due to the increase in space available.**

increased by almost 125mm (5in) and the length by 65mm (2½in). Yet parking is still no problem … Height has not been affected. Thus access to garages and multi-storey car parks is as good as ever it was …'

Despite such variances, it remains clear that the third-generation Transporter was bigger than its predecessor. At the front, apart from the attempt to improve aerodynamic efficiency by making the front panel above the waistline much more sloped, a prerequisite placed on all manufacturers at the start of an age where the contrary gods of saving fuel and reaching ever higher speeds were to be appeased, the size of the windscreen increased by an impressive 21 per cent. Similarly, at the Wedge's rear both the tailgate and the window were much larger, the latter by a remarkable 92 per cent more than that of the Bay. Looking at the third-generation's side profile it was easy to determine that the cab doors had become larger and that it would be easier than ever to gain access to the load, or passenger-carrying area thanks to the generous proportions of the sliding door. Even the engine-cooling louvres were much larger.

Note should be taken at this point that the third-generation Transporter bore more than a passing visual resemblance to Volkswagen's recently introduced larger commercial, the water-cooled LT. Both featured a wide grille, with integrated headlamps and a diminutive VW roundel, at least in comparison with that of even the latter day Bay. Curiously, while the LT was favoured with indicators above the grille, in a similar location to those of a face-lifted Bay, the Wedge hopped back several years, to a position close to the unsavoury girder-like bumper with its nasty plastic end-caps, reminiscent of early day Bays. Volkswagen made good however, by ensuring that at least the indicators were of the wrap-around variety, something that could not be said of the Bay's.

If the latest generation of Transporter looked and indeed was larger outside, it goes without saying that the same applied to its interior. Despite full advantage having been taken of the advances in computer technology that allowed any designer to engineer the best use of space far more effectively than had previously been possible, some of what was achieved was hardly rocket science! As an example, the luggage platform above the engine was much lower than it had been in the Bay, to the tune of some 145mm (5.7in), thus increasing the storage volume by a very useful 40 per cent. Various devices were employed to

of the wheel arches and lower parts of the body. The third-generation Transporter was undoubtedly launched in an age when the gurus of style and design had decreed that chrome and other bright work was taboo, making it in comparison with both the Bay and Splitty Microbuses decidedly austere in trim, or, in the case of other models in the range, a landmark of simple black plastic and black rubber without any form of insert, or similarly painted metal.

On the specific issue of size, short of taking a tape measure to both a Bay and a Wedge, reliance has to be placed on the specifications published by Volkswagen and here there is conflict.

Reference to the technical sections of various sales brochures reveals that at 4,570mm (179.9in) the T3 was 150mm (nearly 6in) longer than the model it replaced (4,420mm, 174in). The difference in width was equally significant if not more so, for the new Transporter rolled in at 1,844mm (72.6in) compared with the Bay's 1,765mm (69.5in), a difference of 80mm (3in). In terms of height there wasn't a great deal of difference between the outgoing second-generation model at 1,976mm (77.8in) and the incoming T3 at 1,963mm (77.3in).

The increase in width was given prominence in the promotional brochures: 'As far as alterations to dimensions are concerned, the width has been achieve this advantage, including modifying the engine's ancillaries so that the cooling fan was attached to the nose of the crankshaft as it had been with the 1700, 1800 and 2-litre engines in the Bay, while other parts such as the coil, alternator and even the air-filter were moved to the sides of the engine compartment.

Volkswagen quickly noted all possible ways of announcing the boost in available space and a quoted release of another 0.7 cubic metres (24.7cu ft) worth of storage capacity. In addition to access through the loading doors being much easier, the computer-designed plan having created a 100mm less exerting step-up into the interior, achieved at least in part by doing away with the old cross-members of previous generations. The total available loading space in a Panel van was now listed as 4.4sq m (47.4sq ft), (Bay 4.1sq m/ 44.1sq ft), with a load volume of 5.7cu m (201.3cu ft) compared with 5.0cu m/177cu ft in the Bay.

A combination of a slightly longer wheelbase at 2,459mm (96.8in), matched against that of the Bay at 2,400mm (94.5in), and increases in both the front and rear track size to 1,570mm (61.8in), compared

with those of the second-generation Transporter at 1,395mm (54.9in) and 1,455mm (57.3in) respectively, made the T3 more stable on the road. Likewise, a 2-metre reduction in the turning circle of the Wedge set against that of the Bay and now standing at 10.7m (35ft), was duly applauded as, apart from anything else, it made parking the larger model easier than it had been with its more compact predecessors. Such an advance was in part achieved by very precise rack-and-pinion steering, but the new suspension set-up was undoubtedly a key factor.

Sadly, for those who yearned for the days of the Nordhoff era and the retention of all elements of Porsche's genius with the Beetle, the most famous of all his patents, the torsion bar, was no more. Increasingly, Volkswagen's competition had been turning to coil-sprung suspension. For the Hanover operation, the cost of producing torsion bars was expensive by comparison, while thanks to their housings, torsion bars took up more space than was warranted. The inevitable result, bearing in mind that the third-generation Transporter was

⬇ **This Pick-up is delightfully original in that it retains its original wheels and is finished in Volkswagen's standard blue colour, which by the time of the third-generation Transporter was rather boringly named Medium Blue. This is a later water-cooled model, as indicated by the second grille close to the bumper.**

→ The simple days of
Kombis and Microbuses
were over. The term 'Bus'
was now in-vogue, with
'Bus L' being used for
upmarket models. The term
was not readily accepted
across all markets, however,
and it wasn't long before
other, more attractive
names appeared. The model
here is just a straightforward
air-cooled Bus!

↓ The LT, launched in April
1975, bears more than a
passing resemblance to the
third-generation Transporter,
which it preceded by a
number of years. Water-
cooled from day one, the LT
was available in a variety of
body styles.

designed in an era when all concerned were only
too aware of Volkswagen's recent perilous financial
position, was a cheaper and in reality, eminently
acceptable form of suspension. Independent all
round, at the front it consisted of double wishbones
with progressive coil springs and telescopic shock
absorbers. An anti-roll bar was fitted to each of
the track control arms. At the rear, the suspension
arrangements consisted of substantial semi-trailing
arms on the rear axle, telescopic shock absorbers
and coil springs.

Another improvement, at least as far as weight
distribution went, was the removal of the petrol tank
from its traditional position towards the rear of the
Transporter to a location immediately behind the
front axle line. Inevitably, at least when full, this helped
balance the axle loadings considerably, although in
later years the location of the filler cap close to a
seam and below a cab door proved many a vehicle's
downfall as rust took its toll. The spare wheel now
sat under the cab floor, secure in its own metal tray
and allegedly another player in the loadings game.
While the reality was that the spare wheel was better
removed from the vehicle's interior, where it had
resided in days gone by, its new location was to prove
somewhat inconvenient.

## Safety First

In an age when the engulfing nature of health and safety legislation was beginning to make its mark, Volkswagen was at pains to emphasise how structurally sound their new Transporter was. What had been added to the Bay over its production run in this respect was carried forward to the latest model, while more of the same ilk was added. The following extracts are taken from longer pieces included in most brochures introducing, and later confirming, the Wedges place in the Volkswagen story.

'Naturally enough, the Volkswagen Commercials were subjected to extensive crash testing. This enabled a well thought out safety system to be built in. First, the impact of a collision is absorbed by the front bumper and transmitted to a deformation element running the full width of it. This element, in turn, is mounted on a forked frame with pre-programmed deformation points in the floor assembly ...

'Door and cab reinforcements, a safety steering column, dual circuit brake system with discs in front and drums in the rear and brake pressure regulation, are all designed for maximum safety ...'

What independent crash tests showed was that not only was the third-generation Transporter the safest vehicle in its class, but also the model most likely to be economically viable to repair. While some manufacturers concentrated their efforts on electronic gadgetry, Volkswagen had retained their belief in sound engineering. Sadly, this approach limited sales in an age when slick advertising campaigns and an emphasis on luxury was unquestionably all the rage.

## A modern interior

Key to potential purchasers of third-generation technology when it came to the Wedge's interior was the amount of space it offered. For the first time it was possible to present the eight or even nine occupants of a Wedge Bus a degree of comfort previously unavailable due to size constraints. Now the anatomically designed, full foam, backrests offered good lateral support, while similarly shaped squabs gave greater comfort to the thighs than the conventional springs of old. Even the most basic offering in the range had adjustable backrests in the cab, while fore and aft movement was similarly increased by 25 per cent. At the Wedge's launch gone, at least for the up-market offerings was the 'dogs-tooth' pattern vinyl so beloved of Volkswagen

↑ In some ways reminiscent of the Splitty barn door models, the third-generation Transporter featured a massive tailgate. However, unlike the old Barn Door, the engine was far from easy to access, entailing the removal of a cover, and the inevitable clutter placed in the tailgate 'boot'.

throughout the 1970s, to be replaced by a much smoother and more easily cleanable material, while in later years cloth would come into its own. The headlining, extending to the window pillars on the deluxe examples of the Bus, and restricted to the cab in some of the more workaday models, was finished in smooth cream vinyl, while rubber matting remained the mode of floor covering in all but the Deluxe Buses.

Heat was generated from the engine through heat exchangers as previously and as such, was largely dependent on engine speed for its effectiveness. Apart from the traditional vents in the cab area, each operated by sliding controls, for passenger carrying vehicles there were outlets behind the front seats facing the rear compartment occupants. Serious attempts were made to improve ventilation and these included fresh air outlets in the rear sections of the front doors, four adjustable ones set into the roof in the rear section of passenger-carrying vehicles, in addition to what was offered on and around the vehicle's dashboard.

Apart from the obvious weight-saving advantages of a largely plastic dashboard, through the use of such material it was possible to create something akin to the fascia in a contemporary passenger car. While the number of controls and dials were few both in comparison to today's Transporters and the then current Japanese offerings, the dashboard layout was well thought out. All models featured an angular binnacle in front of the driver that carefully shrouded the key instruments from reflective light. While the more basic models were restricted to a circular speedometer, inordinately large fuel gauge with a bank of essential warning lights between, the more upmarket offerings sported a clock with a fuel gauge inset at its base. Both the two-speed wipers, with electrically operated washers, and the direction indicators were stalk controlled, while such items as the flip switches to operate the hazard warning lights and headlamps were placed at the outer ends of the binnacle arrangement.

Front-seat passenger/s faced a generous glovebox, but sadly a blanking panel remained the most visual part of the standard specification for the centre of the dashboard, as a radio was still only available as an extra-cost option. Ventilation and heating outlets were generous, extending to the area between the cab seats and below the dashboard at floor level. The non-reflective nature of the dashboard's composition, always finished in black for British-bound models, but

↑ **The petrol filler on the third-generation Transporter is located behind the right-hand front cab door. This example is non-standard, but shows off the location at least to perfection.**

→ **The original specification for the third-generation Transporter didn't include the black plastic air-intake covers illustrated, which were added in January 1981.**

available in brown for some European markets, was a definite boon. Although the two-spoke steering wheel was large, as was thought to befit a commercial vehicle, its centrally placed rectangular horn button pad, emblazoned with the VW roundel, bore more than a passing resemblance to the offerings presented on other models in Volkswagen's range. The old notion of a lorry-style flat position for the steering wheel was finally abandoned.

Inevitably, the floor-mounted gear stick was lengthy, something that was also applicable to the 'T'-handle provided on the automatic option, while both clutch and brake pedals were of a more conventional nature than had been the case with the Wedge's predecessors.

## Negatives

Despite what appears to be an unmitigated catalogue of design improvements there were a few aspects to the third-generation Transporter that proved to be far from ideal, despite the fact that each was wrapped up in something that Volkswagen chose to shout about.

While both the fuel tank and the spare wheel were relocated to the front of the vehicle in an admirable move to 'balance the axle loadings', and in the case of the latter, free-up even more internal space, the location of the spare, contained in a tray under the cab floor and accessed by crawling around under the vehicle on a wet and windy night to change a puncture, could hardly be described as perfect.

At a time when car manufacturers in general were becoming increasingly aware that customers expected realistic measures to be taken towards the prevention of rust, Volkswagen had struggled somewhat with their new generation of water-cooled vehicles. In what appeared to be a laudable attempt to counteract criticism as far as the new Transporter went, wax was injected into the box sections and all welded seams were coated with a thick rubbery material. Perhaps not of great concern to Volkswagen, but with age this substance tended to dry out and crack, allowing water ingress and potentially even greater rust problems than had been the case with either the Bay or the Splitty. It is worth adding that

↓ The Wedge's dashboard was very different in style to that of either of its predecessors, and bore a far greater resemblance to those of its VW contemporaries in the Polo, Golf and Passat. Mostly made of plastic, its key instruments were shrouded by a large and near-angular binnacle, while a large glovebox dominated the passenger's forward view. A radio was still an optional extra at the time.

corrosion protection was improved at the start of the 1985 model year, when some key panels were galvanised, while others were coated with stone-impact protection, and even PVC was used to protect such areas as wheel arches. Nevertheless, an earlier Wedge is a vehicle to be watched!

The Wedge's massive gas-filled strut-assisted tailgate was undoubtedly the most controversial improvement of all. Admittedly, it played a part in the easy loading story and, as it was top-hinged, its substantial nature gave protection from wind and rain when doing it. However, its size and the reason for its size, so reminiscent of the barn door tailgate cast aside nearly 25 years earlier, caused owners and service technicians alike considerable hardship. While in the later days of the Bay a hatch had been cut into the metalwork above the engine, affording easier access to the suitcase engines once they had become a part of the power game, there had been no attempt to seal up the engine lid of old, neatly placed below the tailgate.

With the Wedge's design there was simply no room for an engine lid! Access now was entirely dependent on the removable hatch in the rear luggage compartment, a nuisance at the best of times and extremely frustrating for owners of fully laden campers. What consolation there was came in the form of a hinged licence plate-mounting panel, which, when opened, revealed the oil-filler cap, but for most the old adage 'out of sight, out of mind' was only too true, to the potential long-term detriment of the Wedge's engine.

## The T3 air-cooled engines

A major consequence of increasing the volume available over the engine compartment by some 0.7cu m (24.7cu ft) was that the faithful old sit-up-and-beg 1600 air-cooled engine, a stalwart if increasingly underpowered unit throughout the era of the Bay, required amendment to make it fit into the restricted space now available. As such, it was turned into a suitcase-style engine, as per the 2.0-litre of Bay days, which was mercifully carried forward into the third-generation product. Hence with the 1600, the cooling fan was fitted on the nose of the crankshaft, while the ancillaries were to be found lower on the sides of the engine. Truth to tell though, the 1600 should never have made its way into the larger, and inevitably heavier, third-generation Transporter.

As if to emphasise the futility of placing such a by now feeble unit as the 1600 in the latest Transporter, models destined for the USA were only offered with the 2-litre block. The 1600 third-generation Transporter had a claimed maximum speed of 68mph 109kph) and on the urban cycle offered a thirsty 17.9mpg (15.8 litres/100km) to its owner. Even with the very necessary gear changes being made to keep the vehicle from creating a serious obstruction, performance was far from scintillating. The 1600 Wedge was a tiring vehicle to drive for all other than those whose job demanded a pottering approach of short urban journeys, with frequent stops.

The 2-litre engine, again a cast-me-down from the days of the second-generation Transporter faired better in its new environment. Volkswagen suggested that it had a top speed of 78mph (125kph), but most testers and owners came up with a cruising speed past the halfway point in the eighties. With 70bhp at the 2-litre's disposal and its ability to operate smoothly and remain willing under most driving conditions, it should have been more than adequate to compete with the offerings of other manufacturers. However, a combination of a 0–60mph time of 18 seconds, and fuel consumption hovering between as little as 16.8mpg (16.8 litres/100km) in certain urban conditions and a maximum of 25mpg (11 litres/100km) at a constant 56mph (90kph), in reality the now-ageing engine was only just adequate to meet the needs of the approaching decade.

Both the 1600 and 2-litre engines were inexpensively updated as they arrived for third-generation usage. Hydraulic tappets were one of the innovations and, despite long-held views that they took at least 10 minutes to operate quietly, proved beneficial in that they did away with the monotonous job of frequent manual adjustment. Electronic ignition ensured that the engines stayed in tune longer, while a micro-computer, launched as Digital Idling Stabilisation, assisted with the old problem of the engine cutting out on cold mornings, or refusing to start when hot, by steadying the mixture of fuel and air more efficiently.

## First change in power direction

Some observers believe that it was always Volkswagen's intention to replace air-cooled technology on the third-generation Transporter, presumably when both funds and available engines allowed. What could not be disputed was that apart from the fake grille at the vehicle's front, there was undoubtedly sufficient space to accommodate a radiator! What even the most enthusiastic advocate of change cannot have envisaged at the time was a series of water-cooled units unique to the Transporter – the so-called wasser-boxer engine. However, this is to leap ahead of the game a little, for the first additional engine to be offered in the Wedge was a Golf-derived diesel unit, and most definitely another sluggish contribution to third-generation transportation.

Based on the 1,471cc petrol engine, the four-cylinder diesel was first produced at the Salzgitter factory in the summer of 1975, before a Golf powered by this unit received its press debut in Stockholm later in the year. With a bore and stroke of 76.5 × 80mm and a compression ratio of 23.5:1, maximum torque of 60.2lb ft was achieved at

↓ **Ingeniously, a flap covered by the registration plate lifted up, making it possible to check and maintain oil levels without having to delve under the cover in the Wedge's tailgate 'boot'.**

3,000rpm. The engine developed a quiet 50bhp at 5,000rpm and took 18 seconds to achieve the standard 0–60mph measure of performance. Despite what today appears to be decidedly pedestrian attributes, the diesel engine was more than a match for its contemporaries and providing time was on its driver's side, it could achieve 87mph (140kph), while also offering exceptional returns on a gallon of fuel. Volkswagen quoted around 43.5mpg (6.5 litres/100km) under good conditions.

By the time Volkswagen was ready to install the diesel engine in the Transporter, an operation that demanded its tilting 50 degrees to the left, it had grown a little in size to 1,588cc with a 6.5mm increase in stroke, offering a slight power increase. However, for commercial use the engine was slowed to deliver maximum power at 4,200rpm (instead of 4,800rpm) bringing the bhp figure back to 50, albeit with torque boosted to 76lb ft at a mere 2,000rpm.

As might have been expected, the diesel engine model with its essential ancillaries weighed more than any air-cooled petrol engined Transporter. Sadly, diesel engines up to the late 1990s weren't renowned for their speed or acceleration and so performance was far from earth shattering,

with VW claiming a 0–50mph time of 22 seconds. Compensation, if there was something to pinpoint, came in the form of a wide high-torque characteristic, with over 66lb ft from 1,200rpm to 3,900rpm.

Other modifications required to put the diesel in service for commercial use included a larger flywheel and a heavy-duty clutch, while to cope with the kind of load conditions expected with a Transporter, an oil-cooler was fitted to regulate engine temperatures. A starter motor of increased output and a 63Ah battery, instead of the standard 43Ah, more or less completed the package.

## Water-cooled engines

September 1982 bore witness to the fall of the last bastion of Volkswagen's air-cooled heritage, at least as far as German production was concerned. For it was in this month, for the 1983 model year, that the company introduced two new water-cooled engines offering 60bhp and 78bhp respectively, ousting both the old 1600 and 2-litre air-cooled options in the process. Immediately, some motoring pundits claimed that such a move was long overdue, particularly as, according to Volkswagen, diesel sales had rocketed in its short time-span in the Transporter to account for more than half of production. For Volkswagen however such a move was so sensational that they commissioned a mass of literature to impress potential customers with the benefits of its new-found technology.

Volkswagen claimed that their decision to retain the concept of a boxer-engine was based on their many years' experience, 37 in total, with such units, of which more than 30-million had been produced. In practice, they probably had little option without making substantial changes to the design of the third-generation Transporter, which was after all, a direct rear-wheel drive vehicle, very different in nature to the front-wheel-drive options in the Volkswagen range. Certainly the boxer's compact design in relation to both length and height helped with its installation in the existing engine compartment, while its longitudinal mounting and comparative lightness in terms of overall weight was a major contributory factor to the even-axle load distribution and good-handling characteristics already established in the Wedge's makeup.

Made entirely of light alloy, with a split crankcase and wet cylinder liners, both new engines developed their maximum torque in the medium speed range. Both were more economical than their air-cooled predecessors, with figures of 25.9mpg (10.9 litres/100km) overall being expressed for the lower powered of the two engines and 24.7 (11.5 litres/100km) for the higher. With the five-speed box employed, 0–50mph (0–80kph) times were trimmed to 18.2 and 15.1 seconds respectively, while maximum speeds of 73mph (117kph) and 81mph (130kph) were quoted. The less powerful of the two engines was fitted with a 34PICT downdraught carburettor from Pierburg, while the 78bhp engine was blessed with a twin-choke downdraught carburettor, again from Pierburg. This, coupled to modified intake manifolds and camshaft, went most of the way to explaining the difference in power output of the two engines.

Crucially, air-cooled clatter was a thing of the past, thanks to the engine's sound-deadening water jacket, with noise inside the Transporter reduced by 3–4dB (A), a figure that translates into plain English as a 50 per cent reduction when judged by the human ear.

↓ **If the world had been surprised that the third-generation Transporter was fitted with an air-cooled engine when Volkswagen had virtually abandoned this system, there was a further surprise in store, in the shape of the specially developed rear-mounted water-boxer engine.**

of handling the greater torque of both water-cooled petrol engines.

In what at first sight appears to be little more than material published to update the technically minded on Volkswagen's latest engines, the copywriter summarised the advantages of the change from air to water most persuasively:

'Retaining its flat-four configuration ... we've developed a new water-cooled engine. A powerful combination it is too. 20 per cent more powerful in terms of the petrol version. But more important than that, it now delivers 36 per cent more torque. The proof of both is in the pulling. On a steep gradient, for example, with a full load. Give it some stick here and the response is nothing if not positive. Yet for all this extra output, it's a power unit that remains remarkably low revving. So stress and strain are kept to a minimum even if you happen to be towing. It's no guzzler either. A more flexible, evenly balanced engine affording an increase in mpg of up to 15 per cent. Besides being a lot smoother running, you'll also be pleased to hear it's quite a bit quieter. In addition, we've managed to reduce cab noise by 50 per cent with increased sound insulation just about everywhere. Not least around the engine itself. An engine, incidentally, that's where it's always been. Over the back wheels for better traction.'

Finally, as in years gone by, it is worth noting that US-based customers were only offered the more powerful of the two petrol options (plus the ubiquitous diesel). Additionally and again replicating what had occurred previously, carburettors, twin or single, were banned in favour of a 'unique Digi-Jet fuel-injection system' that, as the name implied, digitally monitored the fuel and air mixture for maximum power output. Volkswagen of America quoted a top speed of 84mph for the Transporter in this guise and claimed a 0–50mph time of 12.2 seconds, and a 0–60mph performance of 17.3 seconds.

Volkswagen also emphasised the fact that 'the water-cooled engine enables the heater to respond more rapidly in cold weather', but far more important was the real savings in the cost of servicing. The first oil change wasn't due until 5,000 miles (7,500km) had been covered, the valve gear was maintenance free, while both the transistorised ignition and the clutch needed no routine servicing either.

Coupled to the new engines came the option of a five-speed gearbox for the first time in a commercial vehicle. With closer ratios, the new box was designed to ensure that the pulling power of the engine could always be fully utilised, together with the best engine speed range to ensure maximum economy. While the four-speed box remained an option, it had been up-rated, with a top gear reconfigured to be capable

### 1.9-LITRE, WATER-COOLED ENGINES

|  | 60BHP ENGINE | 78BHP ENGINE |
|---|---|---|
| Capacity | 1,913cc | 1,913cc |
| Bore and stroke | 94.0 x 68.9mm | 94.0 x 68.9mm |
| Compression ratio | 8.6:1 | 8.6:1 |
| Maximum power | 60bhp at 3,700rpm | 78bhp at 4,600rpm |
| Maximum torque | 103.1lb ft at 2,200rpm (140Nm) | 103.9lb ft at 2,600rpm (141Nm) |
| Maximum speed | 73mph | 81mph |
| Acceleration 0–50mph | 18.2s | 15.1s |
| Fuel consumption (average) | 25.9mpg | 24.7mpg (5-speed box) |

## More water-cooled power

Almost inevitably, once embroiled in the world of modern water-cooled engines, there was a mounting impetus to keep ahead of the competition through the introduction of ever more powerful variations on the theme.

The lack-lustre performance of the workaday diesel, despite its apparent popularity, was a prime candidate for enhancement and this came in August 1985 when a turbo-charged version made its debut. Despite ongoing production for the normally aspirated diesel, the turbo version was described as its 'technical successor'. Developing 70bhp at 4,500rpm, compared to the 50bhp at 4,200rpm of the ordinary diesel, the Bosch turbo-charger boosted the top speed to 79mph (127kph), and provided a quick response action through the gears, while retaining a modicum of economy. At a constant 56mph (90kph) a figure of 35.7mpg (7.9 litres/100km) was suggested, while even with the more complex business of testing with a half payload at three-

quarters maximum speed (plus 10 per cent), the Panel van version of the turbo-diesel still achieved 31.0mpg (9.1 litres/100km).

The turbo-charged diesel remained a successful element of the third-generation Transporter range through to the end of its production. As for the apparently eclipsed non-turbo charged version, this was eventually upgraded in 1987 when the bore was increased from 76.5mm to 79.5mm, while capacity grew accordingly to 1,715cc. Maximum brake horse-power crept up from 50 to 57, which was achieved at 4,500rpm. Perhaps to summarise the diesel story most effectively, it would be fair to assume that the non-turbo diesel engine was more likely to be found in the likes of the Panel van and Pick-up, while the turbo-charged version was at home in the middle ranking ranges of the people-carrying vehicles.

Regarding petrol engine development, the major advance was the inclusion of a 112bhp, fuel-injected engine, with 2,109cc at its disposal. With a compression ratio of 10.5:1, the bore and stroke

↓ **The 2,109cc, 112bhp, fuel-injected engine.**

stood at 94.0mm × 76.0mm, while maximum power was achieved at 4,800rpm. This replaced a 90bhp, fuel-injected version of the 1900 engine, an option that had been introduced less than a year earlier in certain markets. Volkswagen described the 2.1-litre engine as 'the most interesting option', for those, 'who set very high standards where performance and traction are concerned...'. Amongst the key attributes Volkswagen listed were a digitally controlled fuel injection system, branded as Digi-Jet, its free-revving nature, and the fact that it was fitted to a five-speed gearbox as standard.

Finally, to further complicate matters, catalytic converters had begun to emerge as a power-draining source in the final years of Wedge production. As such, a 1990 model year Carat for the British market was available with a 2.1-litre fuel-injected 112bhp engine as an automatic, while in manual form the same 2.1-litre engine developed 92bhp with a petrol catalyser. Further probing reveals that the same engine when fitted to the as-yet-to-be-discussed Syncro model (permanent four-wheel drive) developed 95bhp. Key however to both

reductions in maximum power compared to that of the automatic was the small-print description that noted each vehicle had fuel injection, but that 'emission control via a regulated three-way catalyst', linked exclusively to the use of unleaded petrol was now the order of the day.

## Passenger-carrying product enhancement

The basics of the third-generation Transporter remained intact throughout its 11-year production run, the passenger-carrying element nevertheless went through various specification changes. Volkswagen's once unassailable lead with its people-carrying Transporter was increasingly threatened. Other manufacturers, particularly so the Japanese, were undercutting the German giant on price, while offering higher levels of both trim and gadgetry. Although the Wedge's specification outshone that of the Bay, even in its final years in production, steps had to be taken. Painted metal inside the vehicle was no longer palatable.

↓ **Although the third-generation Transporter was replaced in 1990, a final limited Last Edition model appeared in 1992. This example is No. 331 of the 2,500 examples built. Powered by the 2.1 fuel-injected engine, this Wedge benefits from luxuries such as power steering, electric mirrors, central locking and even a petrol heater.**

Although not available to all markets, the introduction in September 1981 of a special-edition seven-seater known as the Caravelle was a first sign that Volkswagen was prepared to accept the challenge. This vehicle featured two-tone paint, chromed bumpers with rubber inserts, quarter-light vents, and a rear window wash-wipe system, and was also witness to a considerable interior upgrade. Frame-style headrests were fitted to luxuriously padded and trimmed seats, which also came with foldable armrests, the full carpet was produced in velour, additional storage pockets were included, the dashboard was offered in brown as well as the normal black, bars were fitted to protect the standard equipment heated rear window, and the vehicle was pre-wired for a radio.

Following a further special edition Caravelle, again not available to all markets and this time based around special Pewter Grey paint, in September 1983 all passenger-carrying models were re-branded as Caravelles, ousting the more basic Bus terminology, while Volkswagen's general trim designations had been adopted. Hence at the budget-end of the passenger-carrying range there was the Caravelle C, with ample seating for 12. A half bulkhead separated the driver and two front-seat passengers from the remaining nine, who accessed their seats via the sliding door. The seats were trimmed in smooth vinyl, the side panels were fully trimmed and the floor was covered in 'easily maintained vinyl board'. The Caravelle CL featured two-colour paintwork and an element of chrome or bright work.

The eight or nine seater (the difference came in the cab), had cloth seats throughout, a carpet trimmed luggage compartment, lockable glove box, trip-meter and clock, and a cigar lighter. On the more practical side the package included protection bars on the rear window, reversing lights, and opening quarter-lights. At the top of the range stood the GL, a seven-seater, with five virtually individual, but actually interlinked, seats in the rear and two separate seats in the cab. All were finished in velour upholstery and folding armrests were standard. The velour carpet, seat upholstery and the roof lining were all finished in matching tones, while additional insulating material was fitted in the doors and behind the side trim panels. The rear window was heated, protected

by bars and sported a wash–wipe system. A welcome rev counter displaced the analogue clock, but a digital timepiece was provided, while the driver and front passenger benefited from a hinged or removable glass sunroof, and those in the passenger compartment luxuriated in a large sliding metal roof.

By 1988, the range had changed once more, with a name originally allocated to yet another special edition, the inappropriate sounding Carat, topping the list. Here was an upgraded version of the old Caravelle GL, sporting additional features and luxury. Volkswagen's brochure writer found no trouble in filling the space allocated with superlatives.

'The Carat is pure luxury for six ... Passengers are cosseted in individual cloth-trimmed seats that have been designed to soak up the miles. The centre seats can be swivelled and locked facing rearwards to provide conference-on-the-move facilities. All seats have their own armrests and individual backrest adjustment. Deep-pile carpeting is used throughout and this in conjunction with additional soundproofing material ensures that the Carat is exceptionally quiet ... Rear-seat passengers have the benefit of an additional heater to boost the output of the main system. Full air conditioning can be specified as an option. From the driving seat the Carat offers all the features of a large car. Power steering takes the strain out of parking whilst features such as electrically adjustable heated mirrors and electric windows provide convenience on the move. Externally the Carat creates a distinctive impression. Its twin-headlight grille, moulded bumpers, colour-keyed lower panels and alloy wheels compliment the standard metallic paintwork...'

Portrayed as executive transport for seven people, the Caravelle by now also featured twin headlights, moulded bumpers and lowered suspension. In addition to metallic paint, central locking was standard. The velour upholstery was colour-coded to deep pile carpeting and even the side panels had velour inserts. Armrests and open-frame headrests were standard throughout.

In addition to the two models already described, Volkswagen offered the Coach and the Bus. The latter was sold as a shell for converters to adapt to the customer's individual needs, globally described as 12-seat minibuses and specialist welfare vehicles.

**THESE PAGES** The Caravelle Carat, which had started life as a special edition, became the top model in the range in 1988, the undoubted Samba of the later third-generation Transporter line-up. Externally, all Carats were finished in metallic paint, sported twin-headlights, featured alloy wheels (well in advance of most vehicles being offered with such luxuries), plus moulded bumpers and lower panel trim. Power steering, electrically adjustable heated door mirrors, electrically operated cab windows and central locking, all added to the luxury nature of the vehicle. Inside the Carat, as the picture shows, the seats were luxuriously trimmed, individually executed affairs, complete with their own armrests. The centre seats swivelled to face rearwards if required. Deep-pile carpeting and copious sound-deadening material came as standard, while full air-conditioning amongst other assets could be specified. Justifiably proud of its flagship vehicle, Volkswagen liberally endowed the Carat with identifying badges and name decals.

As such, the Bus falls outside the general boundaries of this book. However, the eight or nine-seater Coach was a different matter. Volkswagen went to some length to point out that it wasn't a converted van, but a purpose-built people carrier, with lowered suspension specific to this purpose. Externally the Coach still sported twin headlamps and moulded bumpers, but lacked niceties such as alloy wheels. Inside the two rows of three seat benches were slightly contoured and cloth material was standard. The side panels were fully trimmed in hard wearing vinyl, the floor was covered with rubber matting and the luggage area was carpeted.

Nowadays we take for granted considerable luxury in all vehicles, even if they are workaday vans or allegedly basic family transport. A vehicle without central locking is hard to find, one without electric windows slightly less difficult, at least for the moment. In reality, it was during the lifetime of the third-generation Transporter that this revolution began, inspired by the Japanese and in some instances bludgeoned into other manufacturers. Volkswagen had never been known for over-burdening their customers with wizardry, but with products like the Carat they had achieved a more than acceptable balance between their renowned standards in quality and new-wave luxury.

# Permanent four-wheel drive – the syncro

No story covering the Wedge is complete without reference to what has subsequently become one of the most collectable forms of the third-generation Transporter, the syncro, a type that was launched in the autumn of 1985, with the '86 model year in mind. To infer that the name syncro relates directly to a specific model is erroneous, for what was then the latest technology in permanent four-wheel drive was applicable to all members of the third-generation Transporter family from Panel van to Caravelle and furthermore, was coupled to a number of engines with varying power output.

At the heart of syncro technology was a viscous coupling capable of monitoring and automatically regulating the additional front-wheel drive. A self-contained unit, housed in the front final drive, the coupling was filled with a highly viscous silicone fluid and this acted on the internally and externally splined plates in the coupling housing.

The slightest difference in speed between the front and rear wheels caused the driving power in the externally splined plates to be transmitted via the silicone fluid to the internally splined plates that were connected to the differential pinion of the front axle differential. As a result the viscous coupling started to lock and power was transmitted to the front wheels. Consequently, four-wheel drive was virtually always operational although the degree of power transmission to the front wheels varied according to driving conditions.

While the rear axle was still rigidly connected to the four-speed plus cross-country gear, (G gear), the front axle embodied a completely new sub-frame structure with front final drive and integrated viscous coupling. Special guards to avoid potential damage protected the prop shaft, engine, gearbox and front axle respectively.

Syncro technology was developed for Volkswagen by Steyr-Daimler-Puch. Inevitably, the cost of a vehicle so fitted was greater than that of an ordinary model. Although by 1989 the difference was reduced as the

price of the syncro fell, four-wheel drive still didn't come cheap. Predictably, there were penalties in overall fuel consumption, a typical variance in favour of a two-wheel drive Transporter being in the region of three miles for every gallon of fuel used. Top speed, and for that matter the perhaps not quite so important 0–60mph sprint, with two miles or three kilometres being clipped from the total, were equally affected.

Compared to a standard 'c' specification vehicle, which had an overall height of 1,950mm, the syncro model stood at 1,990mm, inferring only a relatively small difference in ground clearance. However, syncro models were true off-roaders, as in addition to their four-wheel-drive characteristics, a fording depth of 350mm, 'with lengthy passage through water', served to confirm. The following extract from a brochure produced in October 1985 solely to extol the syncro models' virtues summarised as follows: 'The outstanding advantages of superior driving performance are too obvious to be missed:

■ Exceptional directional control particularly on smooth, slippy road surfaces with little grip.

**THESE PAGES** Initially launched in the autumn of 1985 as an '86 model year option, the syncro soon became available right across the range of third-generation Transporters. The secret of syncro success, albeit always a more costly option was what, in effect, amounted to permanent four-wheel drive.

■ Optimum off-road performance and improved tractive power on difficult terrain, unpaved roads and on building sites.
■ Outstanding tractive power particularly on snow and ice and for moving off and tackling steep, difficult mountainous routes, for instance.
■ Essentially neutral cornering with improved safety reserves in marginal areas.
■ Positive influence on braking performance even in winter road conditions.'

## And finally...

Production of the third-generation Transporter made way for the new T4 in August 1990. However, Steyr-Daimler-Puch continued to produce syncro models until September 1992. In March 1992, 2,500 'Limited Last Edition' models were produced. These had 4x2 drive, aluminium 6J x 14 wheels, body coloured bumpers and were lowered by 30mm. Available in Orly Blue or Tornado Red paint, both a diesel and a petrol engine were offered.

# CHAPTER 5
# THE VOLKSWAGEN CAMPER

Throughout the first four decades of Transporter production and beyond, Volkswagen might have approved a company's conversion of its Panel van, Microbus and particularly the Kombi into a camper, but did not manufacture such vehicles at any of its factories. The task here then is to take more than a passing look at the key players in the camper story in Britain, the USA, and, by default, in Germany. Space precludes detailed coverage of other conversions, but where a company is well known, or has played a significant part in the Volkswagen story, a little more in the way of linage is offered.

## Westfalia

Although the long-established, North-Rhine based, firm of Westfalia has been generally credited as the founding father of the motorised camper movement, there is ample evidence that others in Germany were thinking along the same lines. For example, those in Britain who attend Transporter-based shows cannot have failed to come across the 1951 Kombi, supplied by Volkswagen to a Dresden dealer minus rear compartment seats and finished in primer. The dealer immediately despatched it to a local Karosserie, or coachbuilder, where the vehicle was expertly converted into a fully kitted-out camper of some complexity. This camper appears to have been on the road at least two months, if not more, ahead of any conversion carried out by Westfalia.

However, thanks to Westfalia's combination of one-off conversions produced before 1955, and what was launched as the Camping Box in 1953 (a clever-designed piece of furniture that could be easily installed for weekend use and equally quickly removed again during the working week), the company became established as the key player very quickly. From 1955, Westfalia offered full camping interiors as a matter of course and in a period of two years had produced 1,000 such conversions. A fully

fledged camper assembly line was opened in 1958, while shortly afterwards Volkswagen's first brochure to feature a camper of any sorts was offered to its dealers. American purchasers in particular took the camper to their hearts and even more so when the second-generation Transporter was launched in the summer of 1967.

In 1968, Westfalia celebrated production of the 30,000th conversion, 75 per cent of which had been built for export markets. A year later, production was further increased, so that 80 conversions were coming off the production line on a daily basis; while by 1971 an amazing 100,000 campers had been manufactured. Inevitably the oil crises of the mid-1970s were witness to a substantial downturn in business, with sales in the US market dropping by a horrifying 35 per cent almost overnight. While recovery did come and some superb Westfalia conversions appeared, particularly in the era of the third-generation Transporter, the heady heights of the first years of the 1970s were never paralleled, just as later Bay and Wedge production always fell short of the extraordinary figures of the earlier second-generation Transporter.

Having initially simply referred to its product as a Camping Box, or in the case of a fully fitted-out Transporter of 1956 vintage, as the Westfalia Deluxe Camping Equipment, from 1958 Westfalia offered both revised versions with SO designations. As the following chapter details exactly what an SO designation involved, it is sufficient here to indicate that the terminology was designed to identify the evolving pattern of camper layouts available.

In 1958 a revised version of the Camping Box was allocated the code SO22. That the name if not the model designation changed to Camping Mosaik in 1960 was significant, for from this point it was possible to purchase all the necessary component parts to create a fully fledged camper. A further revision occurred in 1962, but the option continued to be described in the same way. In the latter months of 1959, the Deluxe Camping equipment was revised

← It would seem that the whole world has gone Camper crazy, with Splittys, Bays and Wedges appealing to a wide cross section of the community. The German firm Westfalia was the first company to produce camping 'boxes', or kits, and went on to convert numerous Transporters into full-blown campers. A great number were exported to America where they were branded as the Campmobile. The example here is a Helsinki conversion and is a late model Bay first registered in 1976.

→ **Westfalia are generally credited with carrying out the first camping conversion, but the complete interior illustrated definitely predates any such activity. This 1951 vehicle was supplied to a Dresden dealer, minus seats and finished in primer. He commissioned a local Karosserie, or coachbuilder, to create a camper, by which time it was early 1952.**

↓ **The Westfalia SO23 was available from 1959, and set a new standard in design that would remain in place for many years to come. The SO23 was based on the Kombi. This particular example, which dates from 1960, is completely original, even down to the awning!**

and promoted in the USA as the Westfalia Deluxe Camping Equipment 59. Not that far off in the making was the SO23, the epitome of camping conversions and the standard Westfalia would aim to set over the next decade and beyond. The furniture was finished in wood-finish plywood veneer, while doors were either oval or half-rounded in shape. As for the vehicle's upholstery, this was the era of either red and black, or more occasionally yellow and black, plaid check. Awnings were finished in red and white stripes, while the roof hatch, described as a skylight in the literature

and best described as a submarine hatch in common parlance, remained a feature of all fully kitted-out campers until the last months of 1964.

The spring of 1961 saw the launch of the SO34 and 35, both of which featured a cab seat with a backrest that could be turned through 180 degrees so that it became a part of the dining area seating as well. On this occasion the SO numbers referred to the finish of the conversion, with SO34 indicating a white and grey laminate and 35 a dark pear wood. In 1962, SO33 was added, this being the fully installed and permanent version of the latest Camping Mosaik. More changes came in 1965 with the arrival of the SO42 and SO44, characterised by a sprung pullout bed that replaced the older arrangement of carefully laying out cushions. These models also bore witness to the replacement of the submarine hatch with three separate options, namely a fixed roof, a new pop-top elevating roof with canvas sides developed in-house, or a full-length Martin Walter Dormobile roof. The SO42 was aimed primarily at the US market with the units finished in wood-look Getalit, while the SO44, designed specifically for bulkhead models was orientated towards the domestic and wider European market.

The arrival of the second-generation Transporter inevitably resulted in revised conversions and new model designations, while the standard form of elevating roof was hinged at the front and lifted to its maximum height over the Bay's sliding door, thus affording the greatest headroom in the living area. However, the older design pop-top and side elevating roof remained part of the range. The new Bay-based models were designated SO60 (Basic), 61 (Camping Mosaik) and 62, the fully equipped camper closely modelled on the old SO44.

In 1969, Westfalia widened the range of options considerably, adding names to the model variations under the global heading of SO69. From this date customers could request an Oslo (1), Zurich (2), Stockholm (3), Brussels, (4), Paris (5), Rome (6), and Amsterdam (7). Of these, the last three mentioned were the budget models, with the Amsterdam being a walk-through variation. Stockholm and Brussels were the most expensive and were duly kitted out with additional pieces of furniture. New and rather basic Camping Mosaik kits appeared in 1970 and were given the codes SO70 and 71.

Come August 1972 and the debut of the re-vamped Bay, Westfalia launched six new conversions,

again with city names, but all under the general designation of SO72. In a rather belated recognition that the American market was crucial to their success, three of the conversions were specifically angled to that market and had US names bestowed upon them. These were the Los Angeles (2), Houston (4), and the Miami (6), while the rest of the range bore the names Luxembourg (1), Helsinki (3), and Madrid (5). As a reminder, it is worth noting that VW of America marketed the Westfalia Camper as an integral part of their range under the blanket heading of Campmobile. In 1972, a right-hand-drive conversion (based closely on the top of the range Helsinki), was produced by Westfalia for sale in the British market and this was duly given the name of Continental. At the time, one of the most popular series of conversions in Britain was produced by the firm Devon, (see below), and during the 1970s they marketed the Continental as an additional option to their own range!

From late 1973, and with an official launch at the Frankfurt Motor Show, the elevating roof was changed, in that it was hinged from the rear and the accompanying roof rack was now positioned over the cab. Further revisions took place to the various

↑ **Westfalia customers could specify the company's own canvas-sided, pop-top elevating roof from 1965. The vehicle illustrated is a 1967 SO42 model, which was primarily aimed at the export market. Available as either a walk-through or bulkhead model, this is an example of the former.**

← With the advent of
the second-generation
Transporter, Westfalia
introduced a new style of
roof, namely one that was
hinged at the front and
lifted to its maximum
in the middle of the van
over the main living
area. The roof's rear
section took the form of
a moulded, built-in roof
rack with integral struts.

↑ September 1973 saw the official unveiling at the
Frankfurt Motor Show of a new style of Westfalia
roof. Instead of being hinged at its front, the new
roof was hinged at the rear.

→ The interior of the Helsinki, SO76, offered between
1975 and 1979. The vehicle's exterior is finished in
Chrome Yellow, and Westfalia carefully colour-coded
the material to the vehicle's paint, hence the interior
trim is of green/orange/yellow/black plaid.

specifications of each conversion under the general heading of SO73, the models destined for the European market were given the names Düsseldorf (1), Malaga (3), and Offenbach (5). All three US options, SO73/2/4/6, were simply referred to as Campmobiles and were similar to the rest of the range, save that they featured specifics to US taste such as mains and water hook-up.

Between 1975 and 1979 two luxurious layouts under the general banner of SO76 dominated Westfalia's production. These were the SO76/1, the Berlin and SO76/2, the Helsinki. The Campmobile option followed the style of the Berlin, but had an additional string to its bow in that it could be specified as P21 standard, P22 standard with elevating roof, or P27 the Deluxe Campmobile, a model that included an elevating roof as a matter of course. All were finished in a single colour that varied according to the 'P' designation, while from 1976 air-conditioning was an option.

With the advent of the third-generation Transporter, Westfalia introduced what proved to be a particularly popular conversion, the Joker, initially available as a four-seater (1), and a five-seater (2). The additional space available in the Wedge and Westfalia's use of up-to-date materials were key factors. The number of roof options multiplied with the traditional hinged roof being supplemented by a higher profile version, while for the first time a fixed high-roof complete with front facing window and two roof lights was also available. More Joker options emerged during the 1980s and included Club Joker, a five-seater with a full-width rear seat, and the Sport Joker, a more basic weekender model.

During the Joker's production span, teak laminates made way for the latest trend in light grey colour tones. The last Joker models were produced in 1987, but its successors, the California and Atlantic, both essentially followed the same layout. Their distinguishing feature was undoubtedly the use of yet more upmarket and by implication, luxurious materials.

In the USA, the third-generation Transporter camper was again marketed as the Campmobile and with the sole exception of the period 1980–81, when a basic no-frills Weekender was added to the range, was virtually identical to the Jokers, Californias and Atlantics of the home market.

↑ The Joker made its debut with the advent of the third-generation Transporter and proved to be one of Westfalia's most popular conversions. Variations included both the Sport and Club Joker models.

↓ The Joker in all its guises was phased out in 1987 and replaced by the California and the Atlantic. Both retained the features of the Joker, but the finish was more luxurious, while the materials and colours used were updated. The California's graphics were eye-catching.

## Canterbury Pitt

↑ ↓ Described in the company's literature as 'Canterbury's Volkswagen Pitt Moto-Caravan', the conversion was available on either a Microbus or Kombi, the latter missing one or two of the attributes of the former. Canterbury Pitt's furniture has since come to be regarded as some of the finest ever produced. This particular example dates from 1964, and sports the extra-cost option of an elevating roof housing two additional roof bunks.

The name of Peter Pitt is an important one, at least as far as British-based Volkswagen campers go. For it was Pitt that campaigned to have the archaic law repealed that merged campers and commercial vehicles under one heading, each with a speed restriction placed upon them of a painstakingly slow 30mph (48kph). A deliberately provocative trip in 1956 into Windsor Great Park, a place where commercial vehicles were banned, resulted in a court case and a subsequent change in the law. A VW Transporter converted into a camper was no longer a commercial vehicle and thus immediately became subject to the rules governing cars. Equally beneficial, providing the camping components were of a permanent nature and subject to an inspection by HM Customs and Excise, the VW and its cousins were now exempt from Purchase Tax. These changes opened the floodgates for camper production and subsequent sales.

Although Peter Pitt had been a pioneer with his VW Moto-Caravan, a conversion available on the Kombi, Microbus, or Microbus Deluxe, import duties resulted in an unfavourably high price for the Volkswagen, and so Pitt turned his attentions to conversions based on the Thames, Commer and Austin models of the day. However, in 1960 he re-launched the Volkswagen-based camper and the following year merged with Canterbury Side Cars of Romford in Essex. This move led to the emergence in 1962 of the Canterbury Pitt 'Open plan Pitt Moto-Caravan'. So successful was this conversion that it remained more-or-less unaltered at the end of first-generation Transporter production.

Canterbury Pitt's publicity machine wrote of the conversion's main features thus. 'Our "Open Plan" on all models incorporates a full-width forward-facing rear seat for three with window seats both sides, giving a total seating capacity of eight and full width lockers underneath all interior seats ... A side door awning and a 10-gallon pumped water supply are provided with the Micro-Bus and De Luxe models.'

Each fitment, normally finished in dark oak, was particularly well manufactured. Conversions effected on the Microbus incorporated a two-tone paintwork finish very much in the style of the Deluxe offered by Volkswagen, but this was not an option for those customers selecting a Kombi. Inevitably more utilitarian, but nevertheless, most of the omissions from the more basic package could be added at extra cost. The elevating roof option was available on all specifications, but again there was extra to pay.

Following the addition of a walk-through version of the Canterbury Pitt conversion in 1965, inevitably some tweaking had to take place when the first-generation Transporter was replaced by the new model in the summer of 1967. Of most significance was a new fold-down cooker attached to the bulkhead, but which could also be swung out for outdoor use. Sadly, Peter Pitt died in February 1969, and as the arrangement with Canterbury was that his designs were produced under licence, the last Bay conversion surfaced from the Ockenden factory later in the year.

## Devon

Undoubtedly one of the best known of the British camping conversion firms was the operation known as Devon. In 1957, the cabinet-makers J. P. White of Sidmouth in South Devon and the nearby Volkswagen dealership, Lisburne Garages combined forces to produce and market the Devon Caravette,

a camper based on the Microbus. J. P. White was tasked with both designing and building the conversion and from the start worked to the very highest of standards. By 1958 they were producing three versions, all of which made exclusive use of hand-polished, solid light oak. Of the three options, the most unusual and, it has to be said, least popular was the MkIII, a conversion that was essentially a mobile office-cum-bedroom for what today we would refer to as a 'rep'.

The Earl's Court Motor show of 1960 heralded Devon's first serious revision to its range with the disappearance of the distinction between the MkI

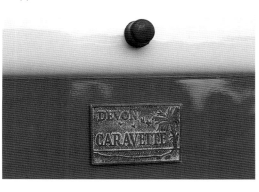

↓ **The Devon Caravette was launched in the latter part of 1960 and, with some revisions, stayed as the top-of-the-range model for the remaining years of first-generation production. This particular example dates from 1963 and features the then latest style of cooker, which was detachable from the door and came complete with an all-round heat and weather shield, plus a warming rack. The cabinet on the other door was home to the vehicle's crockery. Note how the Caravette badge somewhat optimistically featured palm trees!**

Identifying some of the simpler conversions can be quite difficult. To many, this vehicle could well be a Kombi finished in Velvet Green, but in reality it is a Devon Torvette Spaceway. The Torvette replaced the Devonette budget model in the autumn of 1965, the Spaceway option being added across the range for 1966. The Torvette's interior was rather basic, but its appeal was in an adaptable layout that offered a good amount of floor space for load carrying.

and MkII and the loss of an elegant rounded cupboard for a simpler, easier to construct, squared-off unit. In a similar vein to Westfalia, having once amended the product range, Devon continued so to do with great regularity. Unlike Westfalia, Devon chose the route of model names rather than numbers. For 1962 the Caravette was joined by a no-frills budget model, the Devonette. More simply appointed, the new model was available as a conversion on either the Kombi or Microbus, while the Caravette could be specified as either a Microbus or Microbus Deluxe. For the first time purchasers of either model could specify the Gentlux elevating roof, a small pop-top with a fitted skylight.

During 1963, and in preparation for the launch of the 1964 models, Devon discarded the Gentlux roof in favour of a Martin Walter product. This name was, at least behind the Dormobile brand with which it was associated, perhaps the most famous of all British-based Camper conversions, if not necessarily Volkswagen-based products. The Martin Walter roof, a large side-hinged, PVC elevating affair, offered extra sleeping accommodation if fitted with bunks and crucially, 6ft 6in (1,980mm) of headroom over a largish area of the camper, giving the vehicle a light and airy feeling.

The 1965 range, again launched in the autumn of the previous year, saw the Devonette discarded in favour of the Torvette, a model that was still in the budget bracket while offering more cupboard space than that available in its predecessor. Additionally, both the Caravette and the Torvette were offered in two forms: the traditional bulkhead conversion now referred to as the 'Standard', and a walk-through model, named the 'Spaceway'. Of the two, the last named was slightly more expensive, although this was not an option where a Microbus Deluxe was used as the basis for the conversion.

With the arrival of the second-generation Transporter, not only was the bulkhead model a thing of the past, but so also was the use of the Martin Walter elevating roof. The latter was replaced by Devon's own patent form of centrally elevating roof, an item that came complete with two single berths and curtains. Available as an optional extra on all models, its cost was approximately 10 per cent of the purchase price of the new top-of-the-range model.

In addition to the budget Torvette and more luxurious Caravette, Devon took the opportunity to add a new top of the range model that was named the Eurovette. Devon's literature of the day distinguished

→ With the arrival of the second-generation Transporter, Devon quickly added a new top-of-the-range model, the Eurovette. The cabinets were finished in light oak. The units that can be seen here include, to the left, the combined larder, cool box and water tank, and to the right, in front of the sliding door, the combined oven and hob. This unit could be demounted for outside usage and featured a substantial heat and windshield. The table includes an extension flap, while the seats are covered in vinyl on one side and Duracour fabric on the other. The floor covering is of relief-textured tiles.

↑ Built on the Microbus, the Devon Caravette offered fewer standard fittings than those included on the Eurovette. This example has the optional-extra elevating roof of Devon's own design. Before the arrival of the Bay, some Splitty conversions had included a Martin Walter elevating roof.

↓ In the era of the second-generation Transporter, Devon changed the names and specifications of their conversions with alarming regularity. The Moonraker made its debut in late 1970, replacing the Eurovette as the top model in the range. This example, dating from 1972, shows the swing-out cooker and white-faced melamine doors and draw fronts.

between the Caravette and Eurovette by suggesting that the former was built to the same high standard as the latter, but boasted fewer fittings in the basic cost. All three conversions took advantage of the space afforded by the second-generation Transporter compared to that of the first.

Come the London Motor Show of 1970 it was all change for Devon once more. Two new models were launched: the Sunlander, a budget model designed to double as a workhorse and casual weekend away vehicle, and the Moonraker; very much designed to accommodate the dedicated camper. Nevertheless, the Moonraker was available as a conversion on the Kombi as well as the Microbus, just as the Sunlander could be specified on the more upmarket Microbus.

In the autumn of 1971, the Devonette was

reintroduced to replace the short-lived Sunlander. Still very much a multipurpose workhorse in the budget mould, just like the model it replaced, the Devonette nevertheless exhibited several refinements over its predecessor that justified its existence. At the same time, the Moonraker's specification was further enhanced through the addition of what had once been additional-cost extras in the standard list of fittings.

A further year into the 1970s and Volkswagen GB was producing its own literature covering the specifics of what appeared to be their campers. The Caravette was quite clearly a member of the Devon fraternity, while the other model was the Westfalia alluded to earlier and promoted under the name of Continental. Curiously, Devon's own literature soon came to include the Continental, openly indicating that it was built in Germany without making specific reference to Westfalia. For Caravette purchasers the situation was clearer, in that here was a conversion that was intended to run alongside the Moonraker, and as such was witness to comparable levels of trim and fitments. Sadly, like many consumables in the 1970s, standards of quality if not of fit were declining. For the first time veneers were making a presence at the expense of 'real' wood!

For 1974, the Eurovette re-emerged as Devon's most costly conversion and benefited from a further battery of refinements, soon to be most readily identifiable by a louvred side window on the driver's side. As the effects of spiralling inflation took their toll, Devon had little option but to downgrade their offer to remain competitive. Key to this was the emergence of the Eurovette conversion based on the once lowly Panel van and the disappearance of the more expensive Microbus from the list of vehicles on which a conversion could be effected.

In 1978, Devon launched their final two conversions using the second-generation Transporter as a base. First of all the Moonraker made a reappearance, this time featuring a fully fitted kitchen unit, plus storage space, both of which were located on the side of the vehicle opposite to the sliding door. The new budget model, if that term was still appropriate for a vehicle with a by now heavy price tag, was given the name Sundowner – a nom-de-plume not to be confused with the earlier Sunlander conversion.

Although not available at the Moonraker's relaunch, it was soon possible to order the model with the Devon Double Top elevating roof: a full length, side-hinged roof reminiscent of the Martin Walter option of yesteryear. As for the Sundowner, the new 'base model' was only available with single-colour exterior paintwork, was based exclusively on the Panel van, and was designed to be a cross between a people carrier and a basic camper.

The arrival of the third-generation Transporter from Hanover had little real impact on the Devon line-up, as both the Sundowner and Moonraker conversions were carried over from the days of the Bay. After all, Devon like others offering camping conversions had more room to play with in the Wedge. Only two issues warrant a note. The first was that the once-lowly base model had graduated to both 'luxury velour upholstery' and 'carpet trim throughout', undoubtedly a sign of what potential buyers were demanding. The second related to elevating roofs, for now the 'Double Top' became a standard option.

Come the latter months of 1984, and at a point when Devon had abandoned their traditional home in Sidmouth in favour of new premises in Exeter, they added a new top-of-the-range model, the Sunrise, while the company deleted the Sundowner at the same time. As the Moonraker's specification was slightly improved, the pattern of catering for ever-increasing luxury was confirmed. The other major news was that the elevating roof, by now given the Aerospace brand name, was joined by a rigid High Top.

↑ ↓ Devon continued to produce increasingly luxurious campers as the third-generation Transporter progressed from air to water-cooling. Moonrakers were partially eclipsed by a new, more luxurious offering, while the Eurovette name reappeared in 1986 as a fixed Hi-Top. In 1989, the original Devon operation sold the Motorhome side of the business.

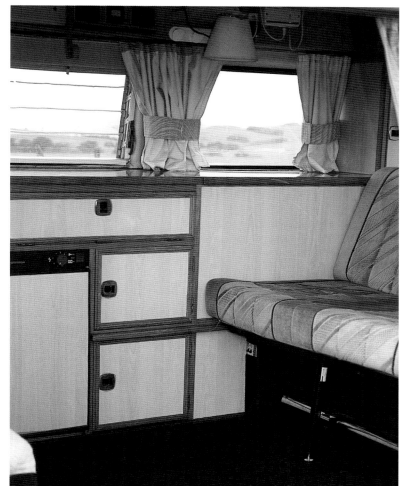

→ Finished in Marsala Red this 78bhp water-cooled third-generation model started life as a Panel van. It was converted to a camper by Manchester-based Leisuredrive.

↓ Cotswold-based Auto-sleeper, still very much involved with Volkswagens and the business of converting Transporters, effected their first conversion on a VW as recently as 1988. The model depicted dates from 1989 and is a Trident, Auto-sleeper's option with a permanent aerodynamically angled high-top roof. Very much away from the norm, this example is based on a syncro.

Devon as a company split in 1989, with the camper element being sold off to new owners. However, before this occurred, there had been one further rather significant change made. Back came the Eurovette at the top-of-the-range, dislodging the Sunrise, while another old favourite, the Caravette, was reincarnated, this time being dubbed as the complete opposite to the top of the market model. Finally, the dependable Moonraker stayed in position, its well-equipped kitchen and desirable list of accessories being appropriately highlighted in Devon's literature.

# An A-to-Z of Volkswagen Campers

### AUTOHOMES UK
Born in 1983 out of the collapse of CI (Campers International), Autohomes UK soon started to produce conversions with the names of Karisma, Kameo and Kamper, the first two of which were designed to accommodate two, rather than four, people.

### AUTO-SLEEPER
A key producer, at least as far as the T4 and T5 are concerned, the Cotswolds-based company's third-generation Hi-Top brought the manufacturer to the attention of the Volkswagen fraternity.

### CAMPMOBILE
Under the Westfalia heading, reference has already been made to the blossoming level of sales throughout the 1960s and beyond of the Campmobile. Indeed, so much in demand were Westfalia's products that after the appearance of the SO34 and SO35 in 1961, Volkswagen of America had to take steps to boost availability by developing its own version of the Westfalia, which it promoted under the name of Campmobile. Later, of course the term was adopted to describe all campers promoted in Volkswagen of America's literature, while a wit somewhere happened on the idea of naming the Westfalia look-a-like kits as Wesfakias, even though the standard of workmanship was comparable with that of the German product.

The Campmobile took the form of a kit manufactured in the USA that could be fitted by a relatively competent DIY enthusiast. Alternatively, kits were available from dealerships already installed on either new or second-hand Transporters. In the company's literature emphasis was placed upon flexibility: the ability to purchase just one item of the kit, or all the component parts of a full-blown camper. Equally, importance was placed upon the probability that many of the Transporters to be kitted out with some or all the package, might well be workhorses during the week, necessitating the ability to offer 'a quick change' at weekends.

Initially, kits came in three forms, ranging from the 'Basic', to the Deluxe, and Super Deluxe. The Basic kit comprised five windows with gear operation (if a Panel van was involved), four ceiling panels, and a whole catalogue of side and door, plus floor, panels, all of which were of birch wood. Seats and cushions were sold separately, the latter being available in either turquoise or red material. A dinette table and one that attached to the door were also offered, while other available items included a clothes closet complete with mirror, a linen closet, and a small corner cabinet; these two last-mentioned items being positioned at the rear of the vehicle. Check curtaining, including tiebacks, all in soil-resistant material, completed the essentials of the Basic kit.

With the arrival of Westfalia campers specifically designed for the American market during the course of 1972, Campmobile kits were no longer necessary. Finally, VW of Canada was also responsible for home-built kits to supplement Westfalia sales. Initially launched in 1963, and similar in their concept to the American kits, nevertheless some elements varied, including the decision not to follow the check curtain route, while additions specific to the Canadian market, invariably revolving around heating facilities were inevitable.

## DANBURY

The first Danbury conversion appeared in 1964 and was named the Multicar. The company took its name from its location in Danbury, near Chelmsford in Essex. Its status was confirmed in the late 1960s when, along with Devon and Dormobile, it was given official Volkswagen GB approval for its conversions. The Multicar was available as a conversion based on the Panel van, the Kombi, Microbus and Microbus Deluxe. By 1966, conversions based on the walk-through option were offered as standard.

The arrival of the second-generation Transporter led to Danbury dropping the name Multicar, and marketing their conversions, whether based on the Kombi or Microbus, simply as Danburys. Sadly, official approval was lost in 1972, thanks to an exclusive contract bestowed upon Devon, but was regained during the course of 1977. Danbury conversions varied little over first the production run of the Splitty, and once more with the passing years, of the Bay. Originally at least they could always be recognised by their simplicity, but when official approval was regained Danbury immediately introduced a deluxe version to run alongside the MkI Standard.

Conversions carried out on the third-generation Transporter saw Danbury head in the direction of producing two distinct models, each designed for a specific purpose. The short-lived Travelette,

↑ ↓ **Danbury's conversions are regarded as basic by many, a suggestion more or less confirmed by this interior picture. The pop-up cooker can be tidied away into the base of the single seat behind the front passenger. The boxed unit at the rear of the end bench holds a sink. Danburys were based on either the Kombi or the Microbus. This example pictured here, and finished in Pastel White over Niagara Blue, is a conversion on the former.**

← Identifying a Dormobile, a product of the Martin Walter Company, is comparatively easy thanks to its distinctive roof. The model shown is an early Bay-window conversion based on the Microbus. (The roof section was originally white.)

↓ Various firms, both in Germany and elsewhere, went down the road of adding a fixed roof to increase available standing room in a Splitty camper conversion. Sadly, in most instances the aesthetics, not to mention the aerodynamics, of such conversions left quite a bit to be desired! This example is a Freedom camper.

↓↓ Richard Holdsworth started converting Transporters into campers in the era of the second-generation model. The company produced some of its best conversions based on the third-generation Transporter, and spent both time and money upgrading specifications, hence the vehicle depicted being the third in the series of Villa models to be offered.

↑ The Leeds-based Volkswagen distributors Moortown Motors teamed with local cabinet makers Bamforth of East Heslerton to create the Moortown Caravan Conversion in 1958. In 1960, they extended the range under the umbrella heading of Moortown Autohome. The standard of workmanship was high. Sadly, by the mid-1960s, Moortown had decided to direct their attentions elsewhere.

← Based in California, the Sundial operation grew out of Westfalia's inability to meet the demand for their products in America. During the 1960s Sundial conversions bore a close resemblance to Westfalia models, although this changed in later years. Throughout, the quality was high.

succeeded by the Danbury Family Estate was much more of a people carrier than a fully fledged camper. The Danbury Volkswagen Series II, on the other hand, could boast an electrically operated, fully automatic, elevating roof, a first in the world of camper conversions. At the top of the new range was the Danbury Showman, described in the accompanying brochure as 'everything you expect from a Danbury Volkswagen Series II ... and much more.'

Sadly, Danbury ceased trading in the late 1980s, although many years later the name reappeared, the new owners offering conversions based on the Brazilian built Transporter, a descendant of the Bay, although still in production in the era of the Hanover-produced T5.

## DORMOBILE

Mention the name Dormobile in Britain and many would assume reference was being made to campers in general, such was the success of the product range developed by Martin Walter Ltd. Volkswagen enthusiasts tend to assume that if a manufacturer produced a series of camper conversions on either a Kombi or Microbus base their business was centred entirely around the VW Transporter. The Dormobile brand will always be the classic example to disprove such beliefs, as the first conversion on a Volkswagen body made its debut at the Earl's Court Motor Show as late as October 1961. By this time Martin Walter had already developed conversions based on Bedford's models, while products from Austin, Land-Rover and Standard were also offered.

Early Dormobiles featured all-steel cabinetwork, multifunctional swivel seating and were instantly recognisable by their side-hinged, centrally positioned, candy-striped elevating roofs. By 1963, more traditional wooden cabinets had replaced the metal ones, while a basic option, lacking the elevating roof as standard, had been added. It wasn't until the advent of the second-generation Transporter that Dormobile took the opportunity to re-vamp their VW conversions. The D4/6 featured a cooker that basically sat under the front passenger seat. In 1970, for the 1971 model year, Dormobile added the multi-purpose, but equally luxurious D4/8 to the range. Towards the end of the end of the decade the company experienced financial difficulties, and as a consequence no conversions using the third-generation Transporter were produced. The company finally ceased trading in 1984.

## E-Z CAMPER

Littlerock, California based E-Z, pronounced 'Easy', started to produce Camper vans in the mid-1960s as a direct result of the lack of easy availability of the Westfalia models. Their products were available through the Volkswagen of America network, one of E-Z's proudest boasts being that they were happy to work on either new or used vans. Bearing more than a passing resemblance to a Westfalia layout, E-Z's literature referred to 'Diamondized polyclad plywall' interiors and a 'man-sized wardrobe', while the rear seat could be transformed into an abnormally large, 6ft 2in (1,880mm) bed.

## HOLDSWORTH

Richard Holdsworth produced his first conversions when the second-generation Transporter made its debut. Based on the Kombi, the firm was also happy to offer kits for DIY enthusiast to fit themselves. Conversions based on Volkswagens formed only a small part of the Holdsworth business, but some of the finest campers from this stable appeared in the days of the third-generation Transporter. The High Flyer, and later the Vision, were High-Top models, while the Villa, later revamped as the Villa 2, and then the Villa 3, were well known for both the quality and the luxurious nature of their fittings.

↓ The German firm Tischer specialises in the production of demountable cabins fitted to both the Pick-up and Double-Cab Pick-up, very much an American idea. Originally offering cabins on the second-generation Transporter in the 1970s, as per the picture, the standard of fittings has always been high. Shower units, fully fitted-out kitchens, and luxurious upholstery are Tischer's hallmarks.

## MOORTOWN MOTORISED CARAVANS

Leeds based Moortown Motors, also a Volkswagen distributor, produced a range of conversions in the late 1950s and the early 1960s. Like the Devon brand, Moortown employed craftsmen Bamforth of East Heslerton to build the interiors, which latterly were marketed as the Autohome range. Additionally, in later years a budget version was sold, which was known as the Campahome.

## SPORTSMOBILE

Sportsmobile, based in Andrews, Indiana, produced its first camper conversion in 1961, and while today anything from a Ford, to a Chevrolet or a Mercedes might be offered, all those years ago it was the first-generation Transporter that was selected as the base. Conversions were soon available on the Panel van, Kombi and 'Station Wagon', or to British ears, the Microbus. Both bulkhead and walk-through models were offered. Sportsmobile continued to offer a series of conversions based on the second, third and fourth-generation of Transporters.

## SUNDIAL

The Californian-based operation of Sundial was born out of the unsatisfied demand for Westfalia campers in America. Initially their production looked distinctly similar to that of the German company, but by the time of the second-generation Transporter, Sundial's conversions had developed a style of their own. Conversions were based on the Kombi and Panel van and were of a high quality, with plenty of customer options and accessories available.

## TISCHER

The German firm Tischer offered a different approach to the Volkswagen camping story in that their demountable living, dining, and sleeping accommodation, piggy-backed on either the Pick-up, or the Double Cab Pick-up. This left the owners at liberty to travel away from a campsite without their weekend or holiday accommodation, and by implication, to use the vehicle for any other purpose whenever required.

## VIKING

Viking like Devon might best be described as a brand name, but unlike its better-known counterpart was discarded when the new, third-generation model replaced the Bay. Motorhomes launched the first Viking in 1970. However, it was 1974 before the

↑ ↓ The trading name of Motorhomes of Berkhamsted, the Viking, was launched in 1970. However, it was four more years before the feature that makes a Viking instantly identifiable, the Spacemaker overhanging elevating roof, was introduced. The interior, also depicted, was trendily 1970s and as such has dated more than many as the years go by. Although the company continued to produce campers into the age of the third-generation Transporter, the Viking name was quietly dropped.

Viking became an instantly recognisable item, thanks to the addition of a substantial elevating roof complete with an overhanging section. The model designation now became the Viking Spacemaker. By this time Motorhomes had moved premises to Stanbridge in Bedfordshire and renamed themselves as Viking Motorhomes of the National Motorhome Centre. Not long afterwards, a further name change occurred, this time to MI, or Motorhomes International. MI produced campers based on the third-generation Transporter, but by the mid-1980s had ceased trading.

## VOLKSWAGEN – AUSTRALIAN CAMPMOBILE

Following a period when Volkswagen in Australia had been unable to import enough Westfalia conversions to meet the demands of customers, they turned to the manufacture of their own model. This change occurred at roughly the same time as VW Australia moved from assembly of CKD (completely knocked down) kits to full manufacture of both Beetles and Transporters. The Australian camper bore many similarities to a Westfalia product and was given the name Campmobile.

Following the decision to revert to CKD assembly in 1968 and the debut of the second-generation Transporter at roughly the same time, camper conversion work was allocated to an appropriately qualified Australian business. E. Sopru & Company produced a range of Campmobiles for VW Australia throughout the 1970s, and also manufactured Dormobile conversions under licence. From a relatively basic starting point, the range developed so that by the mid-1970s the line-up consisted of the Adventurer Basic, the Adventurer Traveller, the Adventurer Deluxe, and the Wanderer Deluxe.

← **The well-established South African firm of Jurgens Caravans started manufacturing a coach-built conversion on the second-generation Microbus in 1973, and named it the Auto Villa. With aluminium insulated cladding over an aluminium frame, the Luton top over the cab is its most distinctive feature. Luxuriously fitted out, even by today's standards, the inclusion of a built-in shower was unprecedented in the 1970s.**

↑ **In the mid-1970s Karmann acquired a licence to build its own version of the Jurgens camper. Similar to the South African product, the Karmann Mobil lacked the extra sleeping space of the Luton top over the cab. With the arrival of the third-generation Transporter, Karmann updated their product, added the Luton top, and renamed it the Karmann Gipsy.**

→ **Built by E. Sopru & Company in conjunction with Volkswagen Australia, Australian Campmobiles featured kangaroo protection (Roo bars); front mounted spare wheels, and pop-top style elevating roofs that ran from the living area to the rear of the vehicles. Although not visible here, a hinged skylight was fitted into the elevating roof.**

# CHAPTER 6
# SPECIAL MODELS

Even before the start of series production, Volkswagen anticipated that the versatile nature of the Transporter, plus its own planned series of model variations, would lead to demand for a whole series of special models built for a particular task or role.

As early as October 1950, Miesen, an established converter of vehicles for medical usage with a manufacturing unit in Bonn, was offering Kombis in Ambulance mode to hospitals in Germany. By 13 December 1951, Volkswagen had produced its own factory-manufactured Ambulance, designated it the official type number of 27, in succession to a Panel van 21, Microbus 22 and so on, and would shortly include it in the majority of Transporter brochures, even asking the artist Bernd Reuters to work his customary magic on its workaday outline.

To most eyes, sales of the first-generation Ambulance, with 481 units sold in the first full year of production, rising and falling to a maximum of 883 vehicles produced in 1961 against, for example, 45,121 Panel vans and 30,425 Kombis in the same year, made a mockery of the vehicle's inclusion in any literature for general dealer release. However, that the Ambulance was included demonstrated that Volkswagen encouraged a whole host of specials, some of which they equipped themselves, while others were given a specific designation but passed over to the hands of specialist Karosserie, or coachwork companies.

To tidy up the story of the Ambulance (at least until the end of second-generation Transporter production), the numbers achieved in the Bay era were always greater than they had been previously. In the 11-year production run numbers peaked in 1973, when 2,023 ambulances were prepared for hospitals in Germany and abroad. Three years later that number slipped to its lowest point, at 1,221 vehicles. However, once again to put the story of the Ambulance into perspective and returning to 1973 once more, by comparison 56,866 Kombis left Hanover, as did 87,849 Panel vans. Total production

in 1973 amounted to some 259,101 vehicles, of which the number of Ambulances leaving the factory amounted to a little over half a per cent!

One further codicil to the Special Model story is well worth noting. Both the Double Cab Pick-up, launched in November 1958, and the High Roof Delivery van that became available in the autumn of 1961 for the '62 model year, started life as Special Order models produced by authorised manufacturers. The Binz Double Cab Pick-up appears to have been available from October 1953 and was designated the number SO16. Although it is estimated that only around 600 Binz SO16 models were produced between 1953 and 1958, and that of this number the vast majority found their way to the United States, nevertheless Volkswagen deemed it viable to create their own Double Cab Pick-up, a move that boosted general Pick-up sales substantially.

The Binz version of the Double Cab Pick-up demanded the supply of a Pick-up finished in Primer from Hanover. The rear section of the cab was removed and repositioned 850mm (33½in) rearwards. A new roof section, bulkhead, and door, were inserted to create the additional cab area. The Pick-up's side gates were cut down to suit the reduced load platform, while inevitably, the storage space under that area was lost. The vast majority of the Binz rear cab doors opened suicide-style and sadly, the work carried out was never entirely perfect, with interior weld seams being clearly visible and in some instances finished paintwork leaving more than a little to be desired.

SO designations officially came into being during the course of 1956 and 1957, with dealers initially being supplied with a full list of the SO models available, including details both of the company authorised to carry out a specific task, and of the conversion itself. Midway through the 1960s, catalogues were available that included photographs at best, or an artist's impression at worst, of each SO

← There was an extensive list of special models obtainable either direct from Volkswagen or through companies given official status as conversion specialists. Fire trucks were available from as early as 1951, and by the following year had been allocated the general designation of model 21F. This vehicle carries a heavy-duty pump powered by a VW Industrial Engine. Many fire trucks have covered only low mileages in their lives and tend to be well preserved – a worthy acquisition for the enthusiast.

← ↓ An officially converted ambulance was available from December 1951 and throughout the remaining years of Splitty production. With the arrival of the second-generation model in August 1967, it is interesting to note that the Ambulance, despite its low-production numbers, was immediately available.

→ ↓ The Ambulance was also offered in Wedge guise and, unlike the earlier vehicles, a good number were sold on the British market. Note that the model painted yellow at the front is a syncro.

← ↓ The origins of Transporter-based fire brigade vehicles dates back to 1951. Undoubtedly the model most in demand was the Panel van-based standard VW Fire Truck. Fire Trucks often saw little use over many years, and fine rust-free, low-mileage examples crop up on the market reasonably often.

option. Additionally, a list of suggestions for further specials was included, but as many of these never acquired an SO designation, it appears likely that most, if not all, were never actually built.

Second- and third-generation Transporters were also available to order as special models, the list of options if anything being even more extensive. Volkswagen itself was responsible for the Ambulance as already established, but also looked after models where the amount of work required to effect the conversion wasn't all that great. Specifically, Volkswagen supplied a fire tender, designated the Type number 21F and based on the Panel van, but equipped with dry-powder fire extinguishing equipment. The German army received vehicles converted for military use that included such extras as canvas 'blackout' equipment for the headlamps, windows and mirrors, a special zipped map pocket in the cab headlining, purpose-made attachments for firearms, and an all-inclusive first-aid kit.

By the early 1960s, it was possible to order well over 100 special models, a selection of which is listed below, both in first and second-generation guise. Before turning to the list, however, one point is worthy of mention to budding enthusiasts today. While the rarity value of owning a first-generation based snowplough, or mobile shop, might have its appeal and could well be guaranteed to attract a large audience at a show, the practicalities of owning such a vehicle are worth noting. Many of the SO-designated vehicles offer restrictions to its keeper.

Their suitability as a makeshift camper, or as a weekend pleasure vehicle has to be strictly limited, while even a Pick-up fitted with an extending ladder would hardly be appropriate for regular use by a Volkswagen enthusiast builder! Heinz Nordhoff was conveyed to his grave in a specially adapted second-generation Pick-up, lacking both side gates and a cab roof, so that as many as possible of Wolfsburg's inhabitants could pay their last respects. Imagine using that vehicle to attend a wet-and-windy VW event today!

## A SELECTION OF SO DESIGNATIONS RELEVANT TO FIRST-GENERATION TRANSPORTER PRODUCTION

SO1 Mobile Shop
SO2 High-Roof Mobile Shop
SO3 Police – Mobile Office/Road Traffic Accident Emergency Vehicle
SO4 Police – Road Traffic Accident Emergency Vehicle
SO5 Refrigerated Vehicle with 140mm insulating board
SO10 Pick-Up with hydraulic lifting platform
SO11 Pick-Up with turntable ladder
SO12 Pick-Up with steel shutter blind access to enclosed storage box on platform
SO13 Pick-Up with enclosed storage box on platform
SO14 Pick-Up with carrier for long pipes or poles
SO29 Catastrophe and Disaster Emergency Vehicle

↑ **This German Police Surveillance vehicle includes a wealth of extra equipment detailed on the M, or Mehrund Minderausstatung, plate. The plate contains basic information such as the chassis number and paint colour, as well as the codes for the extras. These include air-vents in the rear side panels, opening quarter-lights, cloth upholstery exclusive to the German Bundespost and the Police, special radio suppression equipment, an Eberspächer petrol heater, laminated windscreen glass and a lockable engine lid. Finally, the surveillance teams were treated to more than the makings of a camper based on the Westfalia SO72/7 package Trimmings included a wardrobe, a sink with side cupboard and a small flap-down table either side.**

→ **A reasonable number of ex-German disaster support vehicles are to be seen at shows on the British VW scene. The two shown here are Kombis and both are laden with optional and special equipment suited to their roles.**

→ **The High-Roof Delivery Van produced by Volkswagen from the autumn of 1961, started life as a conversion effected by a private company on a standard Panel van.**

↓ **Here is an attractive example of a High-Roof mobile shop. Such vehicles were designated as SO2s if equipped by Volkswagen or fitted out by authorised specialist coachworks.**

| | |
|---|---|
| SO30 | Ambulance with rolling stretcher undercarriage assembly |
| SO31 | Pick-Up with heating oil tank and dispenser pump |
| SO32 | Pick-Up with roller blind access to enclosed storage box on platform |
| SO33 | Westfalia Camper with small roof hatch |

In the era of the second-generation Transporter Volkswagen authorised a number of firms to produce a variety of SO models. These included Westfalia who, apart from producing Campers, were also responsible for taxis, mobile offices and shops, police road traffic emergency vehicles, low loaders and Pick-ups with an enlarged loading platform. Anton Ruthmann produced the hydraulic lifting platform and Autodienst Prometer a hydraulic tipper. Auto-Dunker in Friedberg, and Brown Boveri York in Mannheim, were both responsible for refrigerated Volkswagens.

| | |
|---|---|
| SO6 II | Panel Van Refrigerated Vehicle with 80mm insulating board |
| SO6 III | Panel Van Refrigerated Vehicle with reinforced interior trim |
| SO6 III | Panel Van Refrigerated Vehicle for meat products, with aluminium trim |
| SO6 IV | Panel Van Refrigerated Vehicle for meat products with plastic trim |
| SO7 | Panel Van Refrigerated Vehicle with chiller |

In addition to the work carried out in Germany, operations such as the Dutch firms Pon Automobiel and Kemperink produced some interesting variations on the theme. Turning to the former first, Pon's offered a Pick-up-based vegetable Transporter, a Pick-up-based sheet glass mover, complete with two large frames made out of a combination of steel and wood, to secure the cargo safely, a Kombi-based ladder truck, and a Pick-up-based road sweeper that included rotating brushes. Kemperink, on the other hand specialised in extending the platform of the Transporter, creating a long wheelbase version of the Bay in Panel van, Pick-up (both single and Double Cab) and Camper form. Visitors to shows, particularly those more orientated towards the Transporter, might well spot an example of a long-wheelbase Camper – one of the few special models offering a distinct advantage over the standard specification model!

→ ↓ The SO11, the Ladder Truck, was available shortly after the Pick-up, on which it is based, was added to the range. The ladder could be extended to a height of 10 metres and rotated through a full 360 degrees. The coachbuilder Meyer, based in Hagen, Westphalia was responsible for such work.

→ The Hydraulic Tipper Truck, SO15, bore a great similarity to the Pick-up, at least when the tipping mechanism wasn't in use!

↓ Few examples of the SO19 exhibition or display Transporter (as evidenced by the mass of additional windows) have survived. Businesses used them as a mobile display of their wares, ranging from vacuum cleaners, as in this case, to sewing machines and flowers. Although there was no hard and fast rule regarding the number and size of windows, here it seems likely that a standard side door has replaced what originally would have been a door with elongated window, as per its immediate neighbour.

↑ Various coachbuilders transformed Transporters into hearses, using anything from a standard Panel van and Pick-up to a Kombi as the base vehicle. This example started life as a Double Cab Pick-up and was converted by the firm Frickinger. An extended coachwork frame of sufficient length to house two adjacent coffins was built on the Double Cab Pick-up base. A large rear window was fitted into a suitable loading hatch at the rear, and lengthy side windows, etched with two palm trees and a cross, transformed the look of the vehicle. Chrome hubcaps replaced the standard painted versions, and in most instances the bumpers were at least painted silver.

← ↑ The Dutch firm Kemperink started to produce long-wheelbase delivery vans in 1954, in response to the request of a biscuit factory. By 1959, the conversion, which was based on the Pick-up, had been given official approval by Volkswagen. Both the examples pictured, a Splitty and Bay respectively, have been adapted for camping purposes.

← **This Splitty saw many years' service as a grandiose milk float. Part of the vehicle was refrigerated, while access to the rear side compartment was via a steel shutter blind.**

↓ **This all-terrain prototype with tracks never made it to production, although its intended purpose of conveying people from hotels in difficult driving conditions was admirable. Based on a 1962 Kombi, the vehicle had two steerable front axles and featured brakes on every set of wheels. It is now owned by Germany's Bulli Kartei.**

↑ ↓ The Australian-built Splitty Kombi – all Transporters were known as Kombis down-under – is easily identifiable if it dates from the mid-1960s onwards. Owing to many owners having to clean their oil-bath carburettors daily due to the ingress of dust, a panel high up on the body of the vehicle was selected as the new home for the air intake vents, which numbered nine, were exceptionally long and faced outwards. By 1966, all new CKD kits going to Australia featured twin rows of nine outward-facing vents, as Germany did not have the appropriate press die to produce long vents. Both variations are shown with the yellow van illustrating the single set of longer vents.

→ ↓ **VW of Australia** found an ingenious solution to the dust problem as far as the Pick-up was concerned, these pictures illustrating the changes made. Ten air intake vents were positioned in the peak above the split windscreen (shown looking upwards from the driver's seat in the cab). The air was channelled through the unique, and decidedly puffed-up, domed roof section to the engine compartment. The second picture reveals blank panels towards the rear quarter where the vents would have been on German-produced models.

↓ **Volkswagen of Australia** developed its own unique Container van for the 1963 model year, in the days when full manufacture took place at the Clayton plant. It was undoubtedly distinct from the German-built High-Roof Delivery van. With the return to CKD (completely knocked down) assembly, coinciding with the general change over in Germany from the first- to second-generation Transporter, spacious vehicles were still available, but in a different format. Seen here is the Mobiltrail refrigerated Transporter.

# CHAPTER 7
# TRANSPORTER AESTHETICS, PAINT AND TRIM

Each generation of Transporter predictably, more or less reflects the fashions of the time. Volkswagen could never be described as particularly innovatory when it came to colour, or appearance. Hence, for example, the Splitty Microbus Deluxe, or Samba, was, like its counterparts from other stables, finished in prominent two-tone paintwork and a mass of bright work. Meanwhile, all members of the first-generation Transporter family were sprayed in an array of colours that have undergone something more than a vague revival over the last decade or so.

Even though an early Bay Clipper L might still be adorned with an acceptable degree of shiny trim, the overall effect to modern eyes is somehow less alluring than when faced with a Splitty. With effect from the 1971 model year, the most upmarket Bus became more noticeably two-tone once more, but a percentage of later Bays exhibit such now out-of-vogue characteristics that make a would-be new owner in the 21st century shy away from them as a first choice.

The early days of the Wedge might be judged a low point by today's standards, for not only were some of the paint options to say the best bizarre, but also, as matt black metal and plain rubber became fashionable, a magpie-bright Bus L looked garishly out of place. Fortunately, by the end of the 1980s a further mood change had occurred and to create the Deluxe look it was no longer necessary to splatter the bodywork in chrome. Alloy wheels had arrived, colour-coded plastic bumpers were just around the corner, while paint colours reflected the mood of a move to more sombre times.

## Trim

Regarding external and internal trim levels, an early Panel van was basic in the extreme. Without a trace of carpet, rubber matting sufficed, while 'cardboard' door trim panels and the lack of anything more than

the most rudimentary headlining in the cab area was standard. Perhaps even more amazing, at least by today's standards, was the Kombi, for this passenger-carrying vehicle also lacked any form of side panel trim, or 'load area' headlining. Admittedly, there was rubber flooring in the load area, but the removable seats were hard and basic in the extreme.

By contrast, the Microbus Deluxe, or Samba, was not only luxuriously appointed but also exhibited Volkswagen's ability to produce upholstery and other materials of extreme aesthetic elegance. The Samba's bumpers (until December 1953 it was the only first-generation Transporter to feature a rear bumper), were adorned with rubber strips encased in bright work mouldings. The VW roundel on the vehicle's front was chromed, the 'V'-shaped swage lines on the Samba's front and below the side windows were adorned with chunky bright mouldings, and more.

Inside the Samba, the upholstery was both piped and fluted, the rear luggage compartment was carpeted, while protective chromed rails were positioned around this area to ensure that no accidental damage could occur to the window glass. A plentiful supply of little extras like coat hooks, grab handles, and ashtrays, complemented the use of an ivory colour, instead of the customary black, for fittings such as the steering wheel, the panel controls, and knobs.

The advent of the Bay, or second-generation Transporter, saw the same distinctions drawn, albeit that 17 years after the launch of the first-generation the general level of trim had been upgraded to remain competitive with other manufacturers. A vinyl headlining was the norm for example, even though the Kombi still lacked a full one. This was still undoubtedly the age of vinyl upholstery, with all models' seats being covered with this material. For a comparatively short time the Microbus Deluxe featured two-tone upholstery, but, while this was attractive, it was not in the same league as that of many Deluxe first-generation models. The norm

← The first-generation Microbus Deluxe exhibited the finest in attractive bright work. Note the impressive chrome VW roundel on the vehicle's front, the finely detailed trim on the Y-shaped swage lines on the nose panel that then ran right round the vehicle, the bright trim surrounding the rubber inserts on the bumper, and, of course, the chromed hubcaps.

↓ Opulent velour upholstery, multi-position seats, complete with individual armrests and adjustable headrests, graced the interiors of the more luxurious members of the third-generation Transporter family.

→ First-generation Transporters in workhorse and Kombi form are inevitably spartan in the level and nature of their interior trim. A Microbus on the other hand is altogether a different matter. Designed to match the exterior paint colours, the interior of the Microbus depicted is finished in Soft Green (77). The seats are both piped and fluted, and a bright work trim strip delineates the change in colours on the interior trim. Passengers benefited from armrests, again visible, and the whole vehicle's interior appeared both light and airy.

soon became a kind of honeycomb seat covering, which when offered in black, was easy to maintain, but not so when in lighter, dirt-showing colours. Floors were covered, where appropriate, with rubber matting.

During the third-generation Transporter's lifetime opinions changed regarding what was luxurious. While leatherette seat coverings, once the norm, remained an option for workaday Transporters throughout, the advent of the Caravelle and particularly so the Carat, saw extensive use being made of cloth and velour upholstery and banished even the most luxurious vinyl to the archives. Rubber matting likewise gave way to carpeting, with deep pile being offered to the most executive models. Headrests, once non-existent, and later very much an accessory at additional cost, became standard, just as they did in Volkswagen's passenger range at the time.

## Selected first-generation paint options

The earliest Panel vans, Kombis and Pick-ups, namely those manufactured before February 1953, were available in Pearl Grey, Dove Blue, Medium Grey, Chestnut Brown and Brown Beige. Of these shades only Dove Blue would survive throughout the 17-year production run of the first-generation Transporter. Between August 1964 and July 1967 in addition to Dove Blue, the workaday models were available in Pearl White, Light Grey, Velvet Green and Ivory.

It is also worth noting that a significant number of workaday models were despatched from first Wolfsburg and later Hanover finished in nothing more than primer. This option allowed businesses small and large to organise paint in their house colour/s, in many instances complete with brand logos and slogans. To indicate the popularity of the primer option, in 1950, 3,201 fully painted Panel vans left Wolfsburg, compared with 2,450 examples finished in primer.

Both the Microbus and Microbus Deluxe were available from the start with either single or two-tone paint. From the Microbus's launch to the end of 1955, the options were Brown Beige over Light Beige, or plain and simple Stone Grey. When the Microbus Deluxe was added to the model options

that too was available in Stone Grey, but was also offered in Chestnut Brown over Sealing Wax Red, by far the more popular of the two options. Sealing Wax Red remained a lower body option until the end of July 1965, but with effect from August 1958 the colour was partnered with Beige Grey. After February 1961, the paint colours of the Microbus and Microbus Deluxe were identical, although the interior to which the paint was matched wasn't. Between March 1961 and July 1964, customers chose between Blue White over Turquoise, Pearl White over Mouse Grey, or the Beige Grey over Sealing Wax Red option already referred to. The last options available on a first-generation model, namely those shade combinations introduced in August 1965, consisted of Cumulus White over Sea Blue, Pearl White over Velvet Green, Beige Grey over Titian Red, and straightforward all-over Lotus White.

To further confuse the issue of paint shades, some camper conversion companies not only offered Kombi-based models with two-tone paint, but also might conceivably select shades not from the regular Volkswagen colour chart.

↑ **The paint combination depicted is Palm Green (L312) over Sand Green (L311), an option for Microbuses produced between March 1955 and July 1958.**

↑ This first-generation Microbus Deluxe is finished in Blue White (L289), over Turquoise (L380), a combination on offer from March 1961 to July 1964. Owners sometimes refer to paint colours by their original German name, for example Turkis instead of Turquoise, and appear surprised when the two words are proved to have the same meaning!

↓ Undoubtedly popular in its day, it is not unusual to discover that owners restoring a later first-generation model have decided to change the Transporter's colour scheme to Chestnut Brown over Sealing Wax Red. Sadly, in this instance the vehicle, a pre-March 1955 Microbus Deluxe has a white roof. Chestnut Brown L73 and Sealing Wax Red (L53) were run as a duo from the start of production to the end of July 1959.

## Selected second-generation paint options

After its 17-year run, Dove Blue was finally deleted as a paint option for the workaday models when the second-generation Transporter was introduced. In its place came Neptune Blue, a shade that was so remarkably similar that only when the two colours were lined up against each other was it possible for all to distinguish which was which.

It would be wrong to assume that all colours were automatically updated because the model had changed. Pearl White was still available in 1968, while both Light Grey and Ivory remained options throughout the Bay era. Velvet Green survived until 1970. Indeed at launch the only new colour for the second-generation Transporter was the aforementioned shade of blue.

In 1979, the paint options for workaday Transporters on the British market consisted of Neptune Blue, Taiga Green, Pastel White and Marino Yellow, while Light Grey and Brilliant Orange were available to special order. Of these options, certainly Taiga Green, sometimes referred to by wits as frog green, and Marino Yellow might be classed as once fashionable but now out-of-favour shades.

Turning to the Microbus and the Microbus L specifically, the early Bay models lacked the distinctive look of the Samba. This was in large part due to the application of the two distinct paint colours. Until the end of the 1970 model year, the division between shades lay in the roof gutter. After that date, the colours altered at the base of the Bay's generous belt line, making for a far more easily distinguishable and distinctive paint arrangement. Although not strictly relevant to paint preferences, a later Microbus L of 1974 vintage for the '75 model year and beyond was distinguishable by what looked like an afterthought rubber and bright work strip positioned on both sides of the vehicle to line-up with the cab and other door handles.

At the start of second-generation production the Microbus was available in Pastel White, Neptune Blue, Titian Red and Savanna Beige. The 'L' model came with a Cloud White roof. Later in the Bay's run more variety was offered to modernise, or spice, the vehicle's looks. Although the British market missed out on such options as a Microbus L with Dakota Beige upper body over Agate Brown, the choice was reasonably extensive. The colour options, each linked to a Pastel White upper body in the case of the Microbus L, consisted of Marino Yellow, Senegal Red, Ocean Blue, Taiga Green, Pastel White, and to special order only, Brilliant Orange.

As a complication, US owners reading the above might well wonder what the difference was between, for example, Ocean Blue and the listing in any appropriate 'Wagon and Campmobile'

← At launch the second-generation workhorse models were available in Pearl White, Velvet Green, Light Grey, and Neptune Blue. The example pictured is painted Neptune Blue (L 50K), a colour that survived right through the Bay years.

← Taigagrun (Sage Green) (L63H), is not necessarily everyone's favourite colour! Note the reflector indicating that this is an American-specification Transporter dating from between 1970 and 1979. Reflectors from 1968 and 1969 were round.

brochure. Here they would come across Reef Blue, Sage Green, Chrome Yellow, and African Red. In the case of the first mentioned, the original German designation was Ozeanicblau, the British translation being more literal than the American interpretation. In the same vein, British buyers received a literal colour description in Taiga Green (Taigagrün), while American purchasers benefited from the more easily understood Sage Green.

← Chrome Yellow, or Marinogelb, was offered from 1976 to 1979 on the second-generation Transporter. To complicate matters there was a change of 'L' code part way through the run. Until a given point in 1977 the code was L20A, afterwards the code was L21H.

## Selected third-generation paint options

A launch-issue brochure for the third-generation Transporter depicted the paint options available through outline drawings of the new model appropriately coloured in. For the British market at least, there were 18 possibilities, divided 11 to seven in favour of single-colour choices, the remaining options being two-tone in nature and restricted to the latest top of the range Bus L. A selection of single colours was only available to special order, as were a percentage of the two-tone options. As in the days of the changeover from the Splitty to the Bay, some shades were carried forward from the second to the third generation. As previously, the basic blue hue was one of the casualties of the generation change, with Neptune Blue being axed in favour of the less interestingly titled Medium Blue. Again, the difference in shades was not all that great.

The other single-colour options available were Bamboo Yellow, Ivory, Orient Red, Liana Green and Pastel White, to which could be added the special order options of Light Grey, Brilliant Orange, Cornat Blue, Agate Brown and Aswan Brown. Of these, certainly both browns, Liana Green and Cornat Blue would probably be decreed as dated by gurus of today's palette.

The two-tone options, as already mentioned, were restricted to the Bus L, although both Ivory and Pastel

**↑↑ From Dove Blue on the first-generation, to Neptune Blue on the second, with the arrival of the third-generation Transporter, the somewhat uninspiring name Medium Blue became the standard paint offering on Panel vans and Pick-ups.**

**↑ Two-tone paint, often in bright colours, was popular in the early 1980s. This example is finished in Ivory over Brilliant Orange.**

**→ During third-generation Transporter production, metallic paint became extremely popular.**

White could also be specified for such models. Like the Deluxe second-generation models, the divide between colours lay below the windows and above the door handles on the ill-defined belt line. However, in what appeared an unusual move then and remains so today, the front panel, including the pillars to either side of the windscreen, was painted in the lower body colour. The options were Ivory over the following: Bamboo Yellow, Orient Red, Brilliant Orange, and Agate Brown. Guinea Blue over Cornat Blue, and Samos Beige over Aswan Brown, were to special order, as were the last two colours of the previous list. The remaining choice was Saima Green over Liana Green. Many of the two-tone options appear dated today!

In January 1981, black plastic covers for the engine intake openings behind the side windows (where fitted) marked the start of the move away from metal and, where applicable, chrome, towards moulded plastics, some of which were body coloured. In September 1984, for the 1985 model year, chrome bumpers were finally discontinued. By this time a good number of changes had been made to the colour range, the most significant of all being the introduction of metallic paint, and in two cases as standard options. These two, Savannah Beige and Dove Grey (in reality a tone of blue) were supplemented by special order Bronze Beige and Flash Silver metallic. Also by this stage it was apparent that preference for two-colour paint was declining.

In the final years of the third-generation Transporter all two-colour options had been deleted from the paint range, at least as far as the Carat, Caravelle, Coach and Bus were concerned, while the number of metallic options had increased. The full line up including those colours only available to special order consisted of Tungsten Grey, Flash Silver, Dove Grey, Titian Red, Savannah Beige, Bronze Beige in metallic options, and Pastel White, Ivory, May Green, Capri Blue, Cherry Red, Light Grey, Slate Blue, Nutria Beige, and Marsala Red, in solid colours.

## Camper paint colours and interiors

No attempt has been made to include the camper story in the general description of paint colours and trim levels. Individual manufacturers varied in what they offered customers and often veered away from the standard specification of a model on which their conversion was based. As a typical example, it was not unusual to find Kombis converted to campers offered with two-tone paint in the same style of the Microbus Deluxe of the day. While many appeared to offer colour combinations in line with Volkswagen's, some converters decided to produce colours from a more general palette.

↓ **This Devon Caravette Spaceway, based on a Microbus, was painted in Pearl White (L87) over Velvet Green (L512). This colour combination could have been purchased as a straightforward Microbus, but many campers based on a Kombi were likewise painted in two colours.**

WESTFALIA

FOR
SALE

JOKER

E105 KHK

# CHAPTER 8
# CHOOSING AND BUYING YOUR TRANSPORTER

For a good number of years the Transporter has been the most popular of all older Volkswagens, even overtaking the legendary Beetle in the desirability stakes.

To start with, it was the first-generation model that aroused the greatest interest. There was something special about its happy smiling personality and the fact that a vehicle, which might well have been approaching 50 years in age, could be considered as a reasonably practical classic. Plentiful spares, usually reasonably priced, were available, and here was a vehicle that was easier to work on than most, and one with a reputation for both reliability and longevity. Further, the Splitty leant itself then and now to easily managed engine upgrades, radical customising, and above all in camper guise to the very much in-vogue weekend away leisure-time phenomenon. Inevitably, increasing popularity ensured that decent first-generation Transporters increased in price to such an extent that it made it worthwhile for businesses and individuals to import rust-free examples from the United States and other countries, where the ravages of many British winters hadn't taken their toll. With, for want of a better term, the trade involved, there was a further spiralling in prices. All of a sudden, the Splitty was increasingly desirable but no longer affordable to many people and slowly but surely attentions wandered in the direction of the first-generation's successor, the Bay.

A Concours condition Splitty is now likely to cost its owner at least the price of a brand new family-size saloon from the Volkswagen stable and in some instances, many thousands of pounds more than even the raunchy Golf GTI. Expect to pay a hefty premium for the privilege of owning a pre-March 1955 first-generation model, the so-called 'Barn Door' Transporter, due to their rarity value. Generally, even first-generation models requiring extensive work are likely to cost as much as a two-to-three year old modern car in the deluxe bracket.

Realistically, the second-generation Transporter remains a more practical proposition on today's roads. Overall visibility is better, the driving position is easier, while the pitfalls of 6-volt motoring, a feature of the standard Splitty until the last year of production, are overcome, as the Bay was fitted with 12-volt electrics from the start. Increasingly powerful engines, introduced in the 1970s in order that Volkswagen could continue to ward off the competition, means that today's owner has a reasonable chance of not causing traffic jams on the roads without resorting to a serious engine upgrade. Likewise, while many a camper of the Splitty era might appeal to the eye, by the time of the Bay conversions had moved on, offering more amenities and greater degrees of comfort. Predictably, as the Bay's popularity increased, either due to a genuine recognition of its assets, or as a result of Splitty asking prices, so too did its market value. While there are still cheap Bays to be found on the market, the majority of such vehicles would require many thousands of pounds spending on them to become completely roadworthy in the long-term. Bays, like the Splitty, are regularly brought into the country, while people are investing time and money in restoring examples for re-sale, knowing full well that they will realise the asking price.

Today, a second-generation Transporter in rust-free original, or restored, condition is likely to command a price comparable with that of a brand-new deluxe example of Volkswagen's smaller cars. Examples to restore will obviously cost less, but even so aren't going to come cheap. Long gone are the days of the second-generation Transporter being merely an old VW!

Although the size advantages of the third-generation Transporter have been apparent for as long as it has been in existence, it is only comparatively recently that to own a good example is to expect appreciation totally out of tune with deposit account interest at a bank. Prices haven't yet

← The first three generations of Transporter are all sought after, and particularly so in Camper guise. As a result, prices continue to escalate with many first-generation models now costing much more than the average new family saloon. The once despised third-generation model became collectable as the earlier Campers fell outside the price bracket of Mr or Mrs Average. This example, being a recognised conversion and of high specification, might realise a little more than normal.

reached Bay status, but they are certainly moving upwards, as once again those who haven't been able to afford a second-generation model force the price of a Wedge skywards according to the rules of supply and demand. Unquestionably, the 2-litre air-cooled Wedge in camper guise is the most popular of all third-generation models, with the underpowered 1600 placed a poor second. An increasing number of enthusiasts appear comfortable with a later water-cooled model, and are happy to enjoy the luxuries associated with a product built in the latter years of the prosperous 1980s. There also appears to be something of a cult following for the syncro models, with firm pricing particularly for the double-cab Pick-up model.

Perhaps the price of a brand-new, entry-level, base-model Volkswagen is the most appropriate guide to the kind of money currently required to acquire a top-class Wedge. In this category of Transporter it is still possible to buy cheap and acquire something relatively decent, but the prediction has to be that within a very short space of time this will no longer be the case.

## The Transporter for you

The question of which Transporter is required should be a relatively easy one to answer, even to a novice in the field. Here, it is not a case of deciding between a Splitty, Bay, or Wedge, as the availability of funds in the deposit account will already have played a large part in any such choice. Rather, it is a matter of deciding between a Panel van, a Kombi, or Pick-up, compared to a Westfalia, or Devon camper conversion. Also to be taken into consideration is which side the steering wheel is on, and if the answer is on the left in a right-hand-drive country then is this an issue?

If an owner's main aim in life is to prepare a vehicle for Concours competitions, which model he or she chooses is more or less immaterial. The same might be said of the person who derives more enjoyment out of restoring or renovating a vehicle than actually driving it, while someone proposing to customise a model likewise merely requires a suitably cheap donor vehicle on which to work.

Assuming everyday use, something that seems

out of the question with the Splitty, improbable with the Bay and, to be honest, unlikely with the Wedge, a decent people carrier must be preferable. Regularly using a Caravelle Carat from the Wedge era would undoubtedly be pleasant, but the suspicion still has to be that it would be eminently sensible to purchase a more modern vehicle, if for no other reason than the potential saving in fuel consumption.

However, as many a Transporter will be purchased as a second vehicle for use as a leisure-time vehicle, inevitably the most sensible option of all for most is a camper. Here, the only big question arising concerns originality and purpose-built custom interiors. With no intention to show the vehicle, perhaps the best choice would be a sound vehicle requiring some work to make the interior feel like a home from home.

Finally, in this section, three other considerations spring to mind. First of all, there is the issue of the low mileage, well-preserved and maintained ex-service vehicle, invariably of German or Austrian origins. A Panel van this might be, or a Kombi at best, but both lend themselves to either professional, or homespun camper conversions. Secondly, potential purchasers shouldn't forget that the Bay window Transporter model is still built in Brazil

← For a good number of years now the second-generation Transporter has been a sought-after vehicle, particularly in camping guise. This late-model Panel van is in Concours condition and undoubtedly cherished by its current owner.

and is available in Britain as a Panel van, or as a fully fledged camper conversion courtesy of Danbury, and somewhat cheaper than a new T5 California. Questions have been asked about the longevity of the Brazilian product, which it is not appropriate to pass judgement on here, but it might be appropriate to mention that the latest models now feature water-cooled engines. Thirdly, for those determined to own a Splitty whatever the cost, for some years after production had ceased in Germany the model continued in production in satellite operations. Rumour has it that such vehicles are not as robust as the German-built item, but it has to be for a potential owner to decide whether to take the chance or not!

↓ The third-generation Transporter continues to increase in value. For the moment at least, the 2.0-litre air-cooled option appears to be the most popular, but a late-model people-carrier such as the one shown, appears to fall only second to campers of all ages.

↑ **Well-preserved and maintained ex-service vehicles make excellent purchases, as they also often benefit from a low mileage. The example seen here is an ex-fire service vehicle.**

## Buying a Transporter – from whom?

Realistically, a Transporter bought from a dealer is going to cost more than one purchased from an individual. Rogue traders do exist and a purchaser needs to be wary, but on the whole a transaction is safer when a 'professional' is involved, while a dealer might offer a warranty, or guarantee. There is also the possibility of a finance deal.

On the other hand sadly, many Transporters sold on specialist dealers' forecourts lack detailed history and paperwork. This can be where a private sale is best, providing the seller can offer details of lengthy ownership, or at worst a list of previous owners, service bills, MOT certificates, and all the other documents associated with vehicle ownership. Individuals should also be able to furnish a potential purchaser with his, or her, reason for selling the Transporter.

It is normally wisest to view any Transporter on the dealer's forecourt, or at a private individual's home. A thorough test drive should be regarded as essential and a vehicle rejected if the seller is not prepared to acquiesce to this request. It is best neither to view a vehicle in the dark, nor in adverse conditions, such as wet weather.

## Assessing a Transporter for purchase

### PAINT

Most would regard it as unrealistic to expect to find a first-generation Transporter in its original coats of paint, although a few such models do exist. (The aforementioned service vehicles even in Splitty guise are prime examples and the author knows at least a couple of campers in this state.) Second-generation Transporters, while not abundant, can be found sporting their original livery, and particularly so when looking at examples built towards the end of the Bay's run. A reasonable number of Wedges are still finished as they were despatched from Hanover, although this in itself by now might be something of a problem. As outlined, over the years more and more metallic paint options became standard and experience advises that it has always been more difficult either to touch up such paint with an artist's brush, or for a professional to match a damaged panel to its neighbouring original.

For the potential Concours entrant it is important that a vehicle, whatever its age, is finished in a shade correct to the year of manufacture. There must be no evidence of other colours present, but a silver sticker bearing the colour code and description would be ideal. The vexing question of original paint compared to a top class, professional respray occurs at this point and to be honest, both are acceptable. Concours rules don't as yet stipulate which a judge should prefer. Inevitably, to many a judge a deep gloss shine with a life of under 12 months appeals more than a 30-year-old coat of paint, complete with the occasional well touched-in stone chip and the unavoidable slight degree of fade, particularly if the Transporter happens to sport red panels. But there are those who take the point of view that it is better to reward genuine care for originality than it is to shower points on the entrant who has sufficient funds at his, or her, fingertips to pour gloss on a vehicle.

On the general issue of resprays, potential purchasers should be wary of a freshly painted vehicle. A quick coat of glossy paint can disguise a whole host of flaws, ranging from seam corrosion, to blatant panel rot, bubbling, and all sorts of other horrors. An honest seller with a recently resprayed vehicle is likely to have kept a photographic record of the preparation work carried out. Paintwork bearing a resemblance to orange peel, showing obvious runs, or transparently dull and flat even though recently applied, should be avoided.

A flat, dull, and sorry-looking Transporter that hasn't been repainted recently should not be dismissed out of hand. Providing there are no signs of rust, or other forms of decay, often an application of T-cut or similar, followed by a couple of coats of decent polish, can work wonders. The exceptions to the rule, however, are metallic painted vehicles that have lost part or all of the clear lacquer coat applied on top of the colour. Nothing can be done in such cases, other than to repaint the vehicle.

To complete this section, there are a few words to be said about campers. First, here's a reminder that not all converters chose to produce a finished product resplendent in Volkswagen's original colour scheme, with two-tone Kombis being an excellent example. Unless a camper is lined up for Concours participation, when it should follow the colour-scheme set by the converter, the main message has to be one of glossy protection first and foremost, with paintwork to suit personal choices a close second.

## BODYWORK

Starting at the top, apart from instances where people have caused deliberate damage by walking on a Transporter's roof, the main issue, although not a common one, is of creeping rust in the vicinity of the gutter where they join the vertical side panels. The metalwork surrounding the side windows of both the Splitty and the Bay tend to be more or less rust free, but with the third-generation model there are many instances known where rust has crept from under the window mouldings and on to the panels.

Inevitably, all opening or elevating roofs are prone to leaks and should be thoroughly checked in appropriate conditions. Camper roofs are costly to replace and not all options are readily available today if originality is required. Water ingress associated with the canvas fold-back roof on a Splitty Samba is far easier to deal with than a leaking metal sunroof as fitted to the range-topping Clipper L, or Microbus Deluxe.

All three generations of Transporter are vulnerable to stone chips on the front panel, and particularly so the Splitty and Bay. The third-generation's grille between the headlamps and the water-cooled versions' radiator panel helps in this case! Untreated chips eventually lead to scabs and blisters. Rust also tends to build up in the recess

↑ Some types of elevating roof are prone to leaks, none more so than this style of Devon roof, available throughout the lifespan of the second-generation model.

← Third-generation Transporters attract rust on the horizontal panel behind the bumper.

← When corrosion affects the battery tray, situated in the right-hand rear corner of most models, an ugly blemish appears on the outer panel. The other rear corner can be similarly affected.

→ The seams of the third-generation Transporter were filled with seam-sealer. The material hardened with age, and if it fell out it would inevitably lead to the ingress of water.

→ Panels at the rear of the front wheel arches are susceptible to rust, causing further damage to sills, outriggers and belly plates.

↓ The cab step area and metalwork under rubber matting is prone to corrosion, and well worth checking before making a purchase.

under the second-generation's headlamps, as well as under the windscreen. Wedges attract rust on the horizontal panel behind the bumper, and there are many examples to be seen where proprietary rust-preventing paints have been applied in a vain attempt to stop the rot.

The cab and side doors of all three generations are likely to rust out at their bases, primarily due to blocked drainage holes that have either been neglected over the years, or have proved too difficult to clean out satisfactorily. Water unavoidably accumulates and the result is obvious. Fortunately, as this particular ill is the result of Britain's damp and soggy climate, rust-free doors from sunnier regions tend to be readily available at realistic prices on the second-hand market.

Doors also tend to drop with heavy usage, simply age, or the inevitable neglect of one or more owners. Imbalanced trim lines tend to confirm whether a vehicle has experienced such problems, while in the most extreme cases the sliding door of a Bay can become damaged.

At the Transporter's rear, rust tends to be restricted to the seams of the fixed valance as fitted to second-generation models starting with the 1972 model year,

while the exposed hinges above the engine lid on post-March 1955 Splitty models, and all Bays, are also vulnerable. The remaining side and lower panels of all three generations are worth checking thoroughly.

Should there be rust, or worse holes, in the right-hand rear quarter panel above the bumper of a Split or Bay, it is a sure sign that corrosive acid has rotted the battery tray and as a result damaged the metal. Sills can often be rusty due to corrosion of the vertical panel behind the front wheels. Should this metal be badly rusted, by implication the under-body protection plates, plus the inner and outer sills are also likely to be affected.

The lower sliding door channel (the sliding door only being available as an extra-cost option in the later years of the Splitty production, but a standard feature of both the Bay and the Wedge), if rusty, could lead to the side door falling off!

A visible outline of the inner rear wheel arch on the side panel on either a Splitty or Bay heralds a costly repair, while panel seam rust on the Wedge is prevalent. A sealer between panels was used in the third-generation manufacturing process. Unfortunately, this tends to harden and crack with the advancement of time, allowing water ingress and the inevitable rust. Spilt fuel from a Wedge's fuel cap, located just below the cab door in the case of all models except the Syncro, not only removes protective polish, but also accelerates the deterioration of the seam sealer, with rust forming prematurely. Should a third generation model suffer from any of the aforementioned problems, as yet its potential value is such that it would be best to avoid such a vehicle, repairs being expensive and possibly almost as costly as buying the Transporter in the first place.

The condition of the front wheel arches is important, and both the cab steps and areas under the rubber matting next to the front seats should be checked thoroughly. Likewise the cab floor, particularly as it is covered in moisture-creating rubber, is susceptible to rust. A thorough inspection should be made of the front chassis rails and suspension mounts, as corrosion in these areas is costly to remove. Torsion bar tubes on both the first and second-generation models should not be welded, and again, are expensive to replace.

Finally, if welding has occurred, check that the work carried out is of a good standard and always avoid a Transporter that has been recently coated with a conveniently thick layer of underseal.

## External trim, window glass and light fittings

Although, with the exception of the Samba and to a lesser extent the second-generation Microbus Deluxe, plus the early-day third-generation Bus L, plentiful trim was not associated with the Transporter, damaged items, such as bumpers, can be costly to replace.

In the decision-making process of purchasing a van, damaged or rusted hubcaps can be discounted as those fitted to all generations are both easy to acquire and reasonably inexpensive to buy, although in such instances cheap Brazilian chrome replacements that will rust quickly are best avoided.

Bumpers, either chromed or painted, won't be cheap, while the decision to add US-specification towel-rail style bumpers to a first-generation model involves more than simply bolting the new one on. (Recently, glass-fibre reproduction bumpers have appeared on the market and appear to be of exceptional quality, suitable for all but the dedicated Concours exhibitor.)

↑ **Beware a vehicle that looks like this! When the outline of the rear wheel arch is visible, serious rust has developed between the horizontal and vertical panel joints.**

Pitted chromed door handles can be replaced with relative ease, even when the vehicle concerned dates from the late 1950s or early 1960s. Prices have gone up over recent years, this being the price an owner has to pay for the privilege of being involved with such a popular mode of transport!

The VW roundel, admittedly of an ever-decreasing size, on the front of both the first and second-generation Transporter is easy to replace, but inevitably the shiny versions cost more. Missing name or engine size badges are readily available, possibly the most difficult to find being the plastic ones that adorned the third-generation model.

Amongst the most costly trim items that may need replacement has to be the anodised strips as fitted to the first-generation Microbus Deluxe. Fittings for such Transporters produced before March 1955, and usually referred to as Barn Door models, are available, if not readily so, although a premium price tag for items of this age, and it has to be admitted, desirability, has to be expected.

It is rare to come across a Transporter in need of replacement glass, although some campers, particularly of the homespun variety, may include panes of scratched and otherwise damaged Perspex. The first-generation Microbus Deluxe also featured panes that were not made of glass, these being both the curved roof lights and the wrap-around windows on each rear quarter.

Over the years a large number of varying light housings were offered, many of which were surrounded by chrome or bright work trim rings. Most, if not all fittings, even those for Barn Door models can be located, but predictably, early units in good condition command premium prices. Fittings for the third-generation Transporter in first-rate condition can still be readily picked on the second-hand market. Tarnished or otherwise dulled headlight reflectors of any age will result in an MOT failure!

Semaphore indicators were fitted to home and European models until 1960 and most owners would consider them at best ineffective and at worst dangerous on today's roads. If contemplating purchasing a Transporter of this age, check whether panel-damaging and inappropriate indicators have been added, or if bumper-mounted and acceptably discreet additions have been fitted.

## Wheels and tyres

The style or design and even the size of the wheels fitted to the Transporter varied over the years and certainly didn't only change when, for example, the first-generation model was superseded by the second. For classic Concours purposes it is essential that the wheels fitted by Volkswagen at the time the Transporter was first registered are still in place, and many consider it preferable for a vehicle to be equipped with the type of tyre it would have had originally. As cross-ply tyres were standard throughout the era of the first-generation model and for many Bay window examples into the early 1970s, this opens up the debate about the acceptability of pre-radial technology in today's driving conditions. Many camper vans of varying ages are to be found fitted with aftermarket wheels. A would-be purchaser has to consider whether they are comfortable with such an arrangement, while many a seller will assume that their asking price can be slightly higher if a set of special wheels is fitted.

At the launch of the first-generation Transporter all models had five-bolt, 16in steel wheels, without

↓ **The silver-painted areas of the wheels of second-generation Transporters produced during and after August 1970, plus all steel-wheel Wedge models, are prone to rust, which although not 'life threatening' can be tiresome to rectify, while detracting from the overall appearance of the vehicle.**

1300 kg

any form of ventilation slots and tyres were 5.50 ×
16in. From March 1955, when the first-generation
Transporter was revamped, the size of the wheel
was reduced to 15in and four wide ventilation slots
were added between the rim and the centre. The
correct tyre size was now 6.40 × 15in while 1964
models and onwards, received 14in wheels with
the ventilation slots reduced in size, and a tyre
size of 7.00 × 14.

The second-generation Transporter was
fitted with 5J × 14 wheels until August 1970 and
thereafter with 5½J × 14, while numerous circular
ventilation holes replaced the narrow slots of
old. The introduction of circular ventilation holes
coincided with the fitting of disc brakes on the
front wheels. The second-generation Microbus L
had 185 × 14 radials from its launch, as fitted to all
other Transporters with a larger engine from the
introduction of the 1700 model.

The third-generation Transporter's wheels were
identical to those of the outgoing Bay at launch and
cross-ply tyres were still fitted to vehicles with the
smaller 1.6-litre engine, except in Bus L mode. Later
in the Wedge's production run alloy wheels were
standard on both the Carat and certain Caravelle

models. From September 1986, the option of 16in
wheels became available on syncro vehicles.

While under ideal circumstances all tyres should
be of the same make, it is dangerous to mix sizes
and is both illegal and potentially lethal to run a
combination of radial and cross-ply tyres.

Kerbed alloys are unsightly and quite costly to
repair, and care should be taken to spot buckled
rims on steel wheels, which might imply damage to
suspension components. Badly rusted and pitted
steel wheels cost a reasonable amount to refurbish,
although it is fairly easy to acquire ones in good to
excellent condition on the second-hand market.

## Transporter interiors

### HEADLINING

First-generation workaday models featured a plain
hardboard headlining restricted to the cab area
throughout the 17-year production run. Otherwise,
bare painted metal predominated. The Microbus,
both in standard and Deluxe form, had a full-length
cloth headlining until September 1964, when this
was replaced by white vinyl with a pattern of tiny

↑ **Original-specification
alloy wheels were definitely
the preserve of the third-
generation Transporter
and not earlier models,
and even then they were
restricted to Carats and
certain later Caravelles.**

perforations. A cloth headlining is susceptible to rot through the action of sunlight or damp, while tears are difficult to disguise. A replacement cloth headlining can be obtained, but finding material of the right shade and consistency is neither easy nor cheap. Although liable to suffer tears in the hands of a careless owner, the only other peril to have beset a vinyl headlining that cannot be rectified is yellowing, caused by smoking.

All headlinings were made of vinyl in the era of the Bay, including those of the Panel van, Pick-up and Kombi. Later in the production run, the perforated pattern was discontinued. Third-generation Transporters also, for the most part, featured vinyl headlinings, but towards the end of production cloth was starting to make a reappearance at the luxury end of the market.

Inevitably, many camper conversions include a headlining that wasn't part of Volkswagen's original specification for the donor vehicle and some later examples might even be partially carpeted. Unless Concours is the main aim, a camper headlining should be something that the owner can live with and preferably, like. Beware water staining where some sort of elevated roof is fitted.

## FLOOR COVERINGS

Certainly towards the end of second-generation production, and with the exception of the rear luggage compartment over the engine in the Microbus Deluxe, rubber matting was the only original specification floor covering. Some panel vans might have been lined out with a ply floor in the load compartment and many campers will have been fitted with either the converter's 'original specification' lino tiles, or even carpet.

The general rule in all instances is to lift the floor covering wherever possible, hopefully revealing rust and damp-free metal beneath. Be extremely wary of water clinging to the back of the rubber, or bright orange rust stains. Worn rubber matting can be replaced with excellent quality replicas. A deal of ingenuity is required to replace original-specification lino tiles from an early 1960s Devon conversion.

## SEATS

For many years vinyl was the standard covering for the seats in all Transporters from the humble Panel van to the luxurious Microbus Deluxe. Ranging in the early days from a fine grained grey-black vinyl on the workaday models to pleated and piped upholstery on the Microbus Deluxe, all are susceptible to cracking and tearing in old age. Realistically, the extra stitching employed in the manufacture of the more elaborate coverings suggests that they might well be more vulnerable, but in reality the harder life of a typical Kombi, Panel van, or Pick-up means that all have survived in roughly the same state.

Vinyl coverings were again prevalent in the era of the Bay, although cloth-covered seats could be specified in some instances. During the lifespan of the third-generation Transporter the people-carrying versions of the Wedge were increasingly offered with what looked like hardwearing and comparatively luxurious seat covers. Harder to keep clean than vinyl, and more susceptible to the effects of sunlight, some covers of this type are now looking distinctly tired. For the Concours enthusiast replacing cloth with material of a similar pattern and composition can be extremely difficult. Replacing vinyl upholstery is not a cheap matter, but excellent reproductions of the originals are readily available.

Unless the intention is to show a Camper on a regular basis in a Concours, upholstery, if not the original, should be what meets the owner's requirements. On that basis, the soundest advice that can be given to a would-be purchaser is to ensure that both the seat frames and springs are in good condition.

## Dashboard, steering wheel, handles and winders

Although the main elements of a Transporter's interior have been covered, without the sundry elements discussed below the owner won't get very far.

With the exception of the Microbus Deluxe, pre-March 1955 Splitties lacked anything more than a single-instrument binnacle when it came to the makings of a dashboard. Even after that date, when a full-length dashboard was offered for all models, there was no petrol gauge fitted until 1961. Throughout, first-generation Transporter dashboards were made of metal and although plastic did play a part with some Bay dashboards, there was still an emphasis on metal. The third-generation's dashboard was a different matter, bearing a much closer resemblance to the average family car of the day. Unfortunately, wherever plastic and vinyl is concerned, there is a danger of sun damage, resulting in splits or cracks appearing in the material.

↑ Hardwearing, but often difficult to replace, rubber matting covered the floor in most instances. (Note the wing nut – a primitive method of either removing seats or making minor adjustments to their position.)

↓ The seats in this vehicle were well over 40 years old when the picture was taken. Plain vinyl seats tend to be more durable than the panelled-and-stitched offerings of the more upmarket models, which tend to come adrift with age. Much later velour materials, favoured in deluxe versions of the Wedge, tend to both fade and rot thanks to the effects of sunlight.

↑ Rock the wheel
holding top and bottom
to detect play in the
kingpins and link-pins of
earlier models.

Auxiliary, or accessory, period instruments (an add-on fuel gauge being a classic example), tend to be worth a reasonable amount, while openings for a radio that have been disfigured in attempting to force a much larger CD player into the space detracts from overall values, as rectifying the damage is neither easy, nor particularly cheap.

Steering wheels, at least until the time of the third-generation model, were somewhat larger than ones used in cars, and were aligned more like those fitted in lorries. Originally three-spoke and black, the exception was the ivory-coloured wheel fitted to the Microbus Deluxe. With effect from March 1955 steering wheels were two-spoke affairs. Ivory was offered until well into the 1960s, when it was decreed that the colour intensified reflections and, as such, was unsuitable. Bay steering wheels were two-spoke throughout, although they became larger with wider spokes during the course of 1977. The third-generation wheel bore more than a passing resemblance to the equivalent offering in a Golf or Polo, while the position had become more car-like too.

Early steering wheels can either be replaced or refurbished without too much difficulty, although the costs involved will be quite high. Later wheels should

require little, if any, attention. Many owners choose to fit smaller, aftermarket wheels, and while these would not win favour with a Concours judge, for the camper owner this personalising touch often suits their design for the Transporter.

Door-cards, handles, internal locks, and window winders; the remaining components of a Transporter's interior, all tend to be robust. However, beware the warped door card that can be a sign of water ingress and therefore potentially serious. Also, look out for the rather more flimsy nature of the third-generation fittings, as a broken door button can be extremely irritating if not replaced. Ensure that the window winders don't creak and groan, a sure sign that the mechanism isn't far away from failure.

## Steering and suspension

Worn wheel bearings can usually be detected by listening for a grating noise or whine from the front, or a low rumbling growl from the rear. If the front bearings are suspected then the front end of the vehicle should be raised, supported on axle stands and each wheel spun to check for grating noises.

The wheel should then be firmly gripped at the top and bottom and rocked to check for excessive movement. If the noise test was negative, play in the bearings can be adjusted out, although it may be advisable to apply more grease at the same time. If the rocking test when applied to first-generation transporters reveals correctly adjusted wheel bearings, any remaining free play maybe in the king or link pin assembly. Again, if it's the link pins this can be adjusted out, but if it's the king pins they will need replacing by a specialist.

Later examples of the first-generation and all Bays are fitted with ball joint steering swivels and should be tested for excessive play by levering with a suitable pry-bar. All models have ball joints on the track rods and drag link and these also should be tested for excessive play.

Early examples of the Splitty were originally supplied with ball joints fitted with grease nipples. Sadly, if originality is important, these are now both expensive and difficult to obtain, but can be replaced with the sealed-for-life type as fitted to later models.

Steering boxes were fitted to both the first-generation and Bay models. Free play measured at the steering wheel should not exceed 15mm. Beware of worn steering boxes which have been badly adjusted causing tight spots when turned from lock to lock. Wedges are fitted with a steering rack, while some later models also benefit from power steering.

The torsion bar assembly fitted to the first two generations are robust units but should be checked for rust, particularly on the end plates supporting the two tubes. It is an MOT failure matter if they are heavily corroded, or have been noticeably welded. It's worth mentioning that a clever welder can repair the tubes and disguise his work to make it invisible.

The robust rear torsion bar suspension on the first- and second-generation models rarely give trouble, the only easily replaceable part due to wear and deterioration being the rubber bushes supporting the ends of the solid torsion bars. The rear wheel bearings of all models are non-adjustable and will require replacement if noisy. The swing axle drive shafts on first-generation models also rarely give trouble, but look out for split gaiters where they enter the transmission assembly. However, it

↓ A pry bar is normally used to detect play in the steering ball-joint swivels on later models.

is not unknown for the bolts holding the reduction boxes through the trailing arm spring plate to loosen causing the casings to crack and the threads to strip.

The constant velocity joints on the double-jointed drive-shafts of later models are about to fail if they are noisy, particularly if a clicking noise is heard during cornering. The joints can quickly fail if the rubber protection boots split allowing the ingress of water and grit.

Wedge models are fitted with coil springs front and rear. At the front, the stub axle is held by ball joints top and bottom. The lower ball joint is attached to a track control arm, with the upper joint fixed to a wishbone unit. The coil spring, which should be inspected for sagging or other damage, is mounted between the track control arm and the wishbone, with the shock absorber mounted within. As well as checking for fluid leakage the shock absorbers should be tested by pressing down on each corner of the vehicle. The vehicle should return to its normal rest position without further bouncing. The ball joints and rubber bushes supporting the wishbone and track control arm should also be inspected for wear and deterioration. At the rear, it is advisable to examine the rubber bushes holding the trailing arm to the brackets on the chassis to check for wear. The shock absorber, mounted separately behind the coil spring, should be inspected for leaks.

## Brakes

All models manufactured before August 1970 were fitted with hydraulically operated drum brakes all round. The drums and linings increased in size through the years to meet the demands of increased traffic and the driver's expectation of more stopping power. Apart from checking that the vehicle doesn't lurch violently to one side under braking and the pedal doesn't need pumping to achieve firmness, there is very little to check. However, a pedal which is firm but has long travel usually indicates that the brake linings need adjusting to the linings. Although not a problem in itself this may indicate a lack of general maintenance, so beware. A quick check of any visible brake pipes is also a good idea. Look for splitting of the outer case and corroded end fittings on the flexible pipes and corrosion on the metal brake lines. As a preventative

⬇ **Wedge models are fitted with front coil springs.**

measure against corrosion, some owners have fitted soft copper brake pipes. Although they don't rust they are vulnerable to damage from stones thrown from the wheels. An alternative to copper are pipes made under the Kunifer name. These are made of a copper alloy that is both harder and more resistant to stone damage.

All models built after August 1970 are fitted with disc brakes at the front, giving improved stopping power, normally without pulling to one side. Apart from a scraping noise when braking, due to pads worn down to the metal backing plate, again there is very little to test. Where possible, check the disc for heavy scoring and an excessive ridge around the rim. This usually indicates that the disc needs replacing. Bay window models with 1,700cc and larger engines and all third-generation models are fitted with a brake servo. The standard test for a servo is to pump the brake pedal with the engine switched off and then, with your foot pressing on the pedal, start the engine. The pedal should move down slightly when the engine starts if the servo is functioning correctly.

## Handbrake

All models have a handbrake that acts on the rear wheels and is activated by a separate cable to each drum. The cables of first-generation models run to the adjusters situated each side of the handbrake lever. Bay models have a rod running from the handbrake lever to an equaliser bar under the cab floor that also houses the cable adjusters. The Wedge handbrake is similar but the rod is replaced by a single cable running to the handbrake lever.

## Gearbox and clutch

Volkswagen gearboxes, especially those on the early air-cooled models, are fairly bomb proof, although expect a little transmission whine, particularly in the lower gears on the older vehicles. Check for a vehicle that jumps out of gear, particularly first, third and reverse under acceleration. Difficult gear selection can also be a symptom of all not being well, but ensure that this is not due in part to a maladjusted clutch cable, or a faulty master or a slave cylinder on later hydraulically operated clutches. A slipping clutch is an obvious fault indicating that replacement is imminent.

## Automatic gearbox

Providing the engine is correctly tuned and running smoothly, progress should be smooth with the gear changes rapid, without the engine racing between shifts, or any interruption to the power output. If the gear changes are early or late it may indicate that the primary throttle valve needs adjustment. Also make sure that the vehicle reaches top speed and the kick-down is operating correctly. Check that all positions of the shift lever are working properly. Look at the ATF level and ensure that the colour is not too dark; if it is, smell a small amount rubbed between your fingers to check for a burnt odour, as this could indicate burnt friction linings within the box, or a faulty torque converter. Any faults found could indicate that serious and costly repairs are imminent. Under such circumstances it would be best to walk away.

**↑ ↑ Drum brakes were fitted to the rear wheels of the first three generation models, and to the front wheels of all models until the introduction of discs in August 1970.**

**↑ Disc brakes were standard equipment on the front wheels of all models produced after August 1970.**

# Engine

With the wide variety of power options supplied over the three generations of Transporter it is not possible to detail every possible fault, but a good starting point is to assess the engine's general appearance. A tired-looking engine bay with cobbled-together electrics and bypassed hoses is likely to reveal a variety of faults, especially on a vehicle equipped with a fuel-injection system. However, while a spotless engine would probably indicate a well maintained vehicle, it is not necessarily so. Start by checking for excessive leaks of oil and water. Air-cooled and water-cooled boxer engines often leak oil from around the seals where the valve push-rod tubes enter the heads and crankcase. This is not a serious fault if it is only an occasional drip, neither is a minor leak from around the oil strainer plate on the air-cooled engines. However, larger amounts of oil running down the side of the crankcase, particularly on the left side, might well prove to be costly to rectify. While it may only be the oil cooler seals, more

seriously it could be a cracked crankcase, with oil escaping from the main oil-ways that run under the surface. Worse still, oil oozing from every conceivable place on the engine can indicate broken piston rings or even a holed piston.

Beware then the Transporter with a coating of oil around the engine bay and the back or underside of the lid. Listen for rattles or knocks from the engine, particularly when accelerating hard, but a slightly loose tappet isn't a problem. This is less detrimental to the health of the valves than a tight one, which can lead to a burnt out valve due to it not seating properly. However, when the vehicle is revved a heavier knocking or low rumble may be the result of worn big end or main crankshaft bearings. A chuffing noise on air-cooled engines can indicate a loose cylinder head due to the studs pulling out of the crankcase. This can also happen to the water-cooled boxer engine, due to corroded head studs caused by using an anti-freeze without a corrosion inhibiter.

Air-cooled 1,600cc engines are also notorious for cracking their cylinder heads, in extreme cases

↓ The 30bhp engine, introduced in December 1953, remained unchanged until May 1959. The picture illustrates the engine as fitted to a post-March 1955 Transporter, with the oil bath cleaner moved to the left due to the reduced height of the new engine compartment.

leading to a valve seat working loose. Another good indicator of a tired air-cooled engine is excessive crankshaft end float. Check this with the engine cold and switched off by gripping the crankshaft pulley with both hands and pushing and pulling. If you can see and feel movement then it's virtually guaranteed that the engine is past its prime. The factory end float setting for all Volkswagen flat-four engines is between 0.07mm and 0.13mm, which is barely perceptible.

As the diesel engine has a toothed belt to drive the camshaft that should be checked every 20,000 miles and replaced if there are signs of wear. It is wise to inspect the available service history and be wary if this isn't available. Another potential problem is the crankshaft pulley working loose and losing the valve timing. This is usually caused by an inexperienced mechanic removing the centre bolt holding the pulley hub to the crankshaft during a cam-belt change instead of removing the four bolts holding the pulley to the hub. Diesel-powered models should also be checked for excessive exhaust smoke during hard acceleration. As with the air-cooled engines, knocking and rumbling when revved could be the early signs of bearing failure.

Air-cooled models with Beetle-derived engines rely on the generator belt to provide drive to the cooling fan. A slipping belt can cause a reduction in cooling air to the engine, resulting in cracked heads and burnt pistons. It should also be pointed out that incorrect ignition timing can also cause overheating due to pre-ignition. Some owners remove the thermostat and the cooling flaps from the lower part of the fan housing, believing that it will increase cooling air to the engine. This is a myth, as the flaps are angled to direct the cooling air towards the hottest part of the engine, the cylinder heads. Therefore, it is worth checking that the thermostat is still in place. It is situated on the right-hand side of the engine and can be viewed above the tin-ware panel between the heat exchanger and the crankcase. On pre-1963 vehicles the heater control will need to be in the off position to lower the flaps, allowing a view of the thermostat.

To prevent icing problems during the winter months with the single carburettor fitted to Beetle-derived Transporter engines, an inlet manifold with a preheat pipe was used. This

can corrode, allowing fumes into the vehicle, or block up with carbon leading to a misfire due to carburettor icing. Taking great care due to the heat involved, check that the pre-heat pipe has warmed up after the engine has run for a few minutes. Later twin-port manifolds can leak air around the rubber boots separating the three sections, leading to a weakened mixture. This can sometimes be detected by a hissing sound.

## Exhaust system

Transporters fitted with Beetle-derived engines benefit from simple exhaust systems that consist of heater boxes or heat exchangers connected to the front cylinders, plus an easily replaced silencer box attached directly to the rear cylinders and the back of the heater boxes or exchangers. A separate tailpipe section is connected to the silencer box. An otherwise sound vehicle should not be dismissed due to a defective system as it is relatively cheap to buy. However, later Wedges were fitted with ever more complicated systems, consisting of multiple sections, which are consequently more expensive.

↑ **Partially hiding behind the aftermarket silver heater pipe is the inlet manifold pre-heat pipe. This pipe often becomes blocked with carbon, sometimes leading to the carburettor icing up during the colder months.**

↑ The exhaust system shown is on a rare early model and as such would be both difficult to locate and cost a great deal of money. However, most air-cooled engine exhausts are relatively cheap, as well as being comparatively simple and, as a result, fairly straightforward to fit.

## Fuel systems

The carburettors of the earliest models are usually less troublesome than those fitted to later vehicles loaded with emission control devices. The early versions sometimes suffer with worn throttle bearings that can be detected by trying to rock the spindle. This can lead to a weaker mixture due to extra air entering the system and even fuel leaks. While on the subject of fuel, all flexible fuel pipes should be in good condition and fitted with proper fuel hose clips. As well as the throttle spindles, later carburettors can suffer all manner of ills due to a combination of more complex design coupled to wear and tear.

Check that the engine runs smoothly from start up and when the automatic choke turns off, that it doesn't stall. Later engines with the complicated carburettors often stall at the first stop after start up and then run happily for the rest of the day. Twin carburettors on the larger engines fitted to Bays and Wedges are relatively trouble free if they are adjusted correctly, while the fuel injection systems fitted to later models give very little trouble.

## Wiring

If all the wiring appears as Volkswagen intended and all electrical components and lights work correctly then usually all is well. The bulk of the wiring, the fuse box, and on later models the relay panel, are situated under the dashboard. Early first-generation models have a twin fuse box to protect the main beam headlights on the front bulkhead of the engine compartment. They also have a simple instrument binnacle surrounding the steering column. Soon, a four-fuse box adding protection to the dip beam circuits was provided before being replaced by a box with six fuses under a full-width dashboard. At the end of Splitty production a box with eight fuses was used and 12-volt electrics appeared for the first time.

When checking wiring, beware of a conundrum of wires, usually all the same non-standard colour accompanied by a forest of insulated crimped terminals. Also be very wary if you find makeshift repairs using tap connectors, often known as scotch-lock connectors. They are often used to bypass standard wiring and very often the fuse box. They are only meant to be a get-you-home remedy and should be replaced and the original fault rectified at the earliest opportunity, as they invariably fail after a short length of service.

Good workshop manuals show conventional wiring diagrams up to August 1972, but, as the wiring and components became more complex as the years rolled on, these were replaced by harder-to-follow current flow charts. Wedge models follow the modern practice using multi-plugs with each terminal numbered. The numbers aid circuit tracing, as they correspond with the numbers used in the current flow charts. In most cases, when replacing components it is a simple matter of disconnecting a multi-plug, with difficulties only arising when an individual pin in a multi-plug burns out or corrodes. This is usually due to inexperience such as connecting powerful auxiliary lights to the main beam headlight circuit without using a relay to protect the original circuit.

When checking over a prospective purchase it is a good idea to ensure that the ignition warning light illuminates when the ignition is switched on and extinguishes as soon as the engine fires. Likewise the oil pressure light. The ignition light, on early 6-volt vehicles often glows faintly, especially at night when all the lights and windscreen wipers are on and is usually nothing to be concerned about, as voltage drop is the cause. However, if the ignition light comes on brightly when driving, it's advisable to pull over as the generator drive belt may have snapped, something that causes the loss of drive to the cooling fan on engines derived from the Beetle unit.

Early vehicles have very little wiring in the engine compartment but the insulation often becomes brittle due to engine heat. The wire to the oil pressure light sender unit is particularly vulnerable to this. Faulty electrical equipment should be reflected in the asking price as some items are quite expensive.

## Battery

Most models, including diesel-powered Wedges have the battery situated on the right-hand side of the engine compartment. Petrol engine Wedges have the battery concealed under the right-hand cab seat. A battery with badly corroded terminals is likely to be near the end of its working life. Beware of the Transporter with an already warmed up engine, it may be hiding starting difficulties.

**↓ The fuse box and relay console is always located to the left-hand side under the dash regardless of the location of the steering column.**

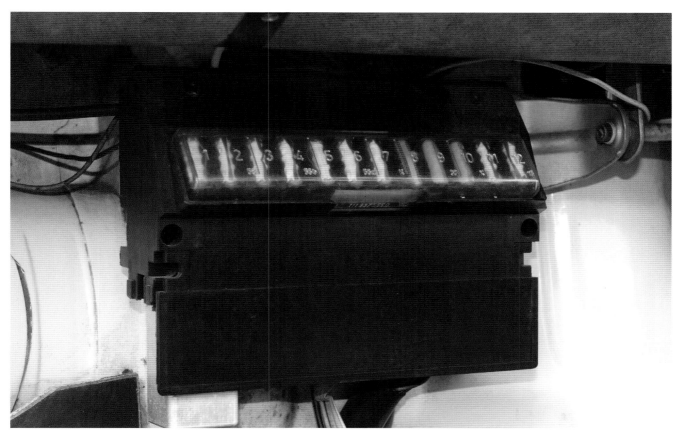

# CHAPTER 9
# CARING FOR YOUR TRANSPORTER

While not wishing to repeat the advice given in the Haynes Workshop manuals, there are a few relatively straightforward procedures you may wish to carry out to keep your Transporter running sweetly.

## Engine

One of the simplest but most important weekly tasks you should carry out is to check the engine oil level. This is especially true with the air-cooled models as the oil, being a vital part of the engine cooling system, needs to be at, or very near to, the maximum allowed level. All the air-cooled engines borrowed from the Beetle range, whether it's the lowly 1,131cc unit found in the earliest vehicle, or the more sophisticated 1,584cc, twin-port motor found in Bay-window models during the 1970s, have their dipstick located to the right of the main crankshaft pulley when viewed from the rear.

These engines are famous for using very little oil between services when in new condition, but older ones need frequent checking as a sudden increase in consumption could be leading to expensive mechanical problems within the engine. The original recommendation from Volkswagen was to use SAE 30HD monograde oil and some owners still doggedly carry on with this. Modern thinking, however, suggests good-quality SAE 15w40 multi-grade oil as an acceptable alternative, as this covers a wider range of ambient temperatures.

Volkswagen used a concave oil thrower plate in place of an oil seal behind the crankshaft pulley. This plate flicks the oil back into the crankcase so it is vital that you don't overfill the engine, unless you want to spray the engine bay of your pride and joy with a coating of oil. To avoid overfilling, the oil level should be checked when the engine is cold and the vehicle is standing on level ground. Top up with your usual grade of oil to the top mark on the dipstick. All engine options referred to in this book require approximately one litre of oil to top up between the minimum and maximum marks on the dipstick. The oil filler cap is situated to the right of the generator and the angle of the tube makes it somewhat awkward to top up without spillage. A suitable funnel or pouring jug is to be recommended to avoid making an oily mess. As part of your maintenance schedule, the oil should be changed every 3,000 miles (5,000km). Drain the oil from a warm engine by either removing the drain plug, if fitted, or the six bolts holding the oil strainer plate on the underside of the engine. The mesh oil strainer should be removed and thoroughly cleaned with petrol or replaced and new gaskets used when refitting. Obtain the correct gaskets before starting this operation, bearing in mind that the 25 and 30bhp engines have a smaller diameter oil strainer than later units. Do not over-tighten the six nuts holding the oil strainer and cover plate.

The oil-bath air filter fitted to early engines should be cleaned out and refilled with fresh oil during a engine oil change service. Replace the paper filter on later engines according to the recommended service schedule.

In August 1971, at the start of the 1972 model year, the 1,700cc engine that originally powered the VW 411 became available as an option in Europe and standard equipment in the USA. The capacity was later increased to 1,800cc and eventually 2 litres. This power unit, often referred to as the Type 4 engine, was also nicknamed the suitcase engine, due to the fan assembly being mounted directly on the end of the crankshaft. This engine is an altogether stronger unit as the crankcase is made of aluminium instead of the magnesium alloy used for the Type 1 motor. The oil dipstick and filler cap are positioned near the rear of the engine bay to the right of the crankshaft pulley. The oil drain plug is separate from the oil strainer plate and a spin-on oil filter is fitted. The oil strainer and plate on this engine only require cleaning every 20,000-miles.

← **After raising the vehicle with a jack, the use of proper axle stands is essential before venturing underneath to carry out maintenance work.**

Great care should be exercised when replacing the central oil strainer bolt as the thread is easily damaged. The service period for an engine oil change is 3,000 miles (5,000km), and the spin-on oil filter should be changed every 6,000 miles.

When the third-generation Transporter was introduced for the 1980 model year, it was still fitted with an air-cooled engine. The options were either a modified version of the 2-litre engine, introduced for the 1976 model year second-generation Transporter, and now designated the CU series, featuring maintenance-free hydraulic tappets to lift the valves, or the sometimes troublesome 1,600cc CT series, suitcase-style engine. The CT engine was also fitted with maintenance-free hydraulic tappets that were often reluctant to fill with oil, resulting in a rattly engine for several minutes after starting up.

From September 1980, a diesel engine became available, with a turbo-diesel joining the model list later on. The diesel models were identified by having two grilles at the front of the vehicle, a feature soon to appear on all models once water-cooled boxer engines were introduced. The diesel engine was the in-line, four-cylinder unit originally introduced in the MkI Golf, and, at only 50bhp in its normally aspirated form, the performance was uninspiring. The addition of a turbo-charger gave it a much needed boost. To fit in the space available the diesel engine was tilted a long way from vertical. Regular oil changes and spin-on filter replacement should be performed in accordance with the recommended service schedule. The drain plug sealing washer should be replaced at each oil change.

In September 1982, a little way into the 1983 model year, the air-cooled options were finally abandoned in favour of a new series of water-cooled boxer engines. These were loosely based on the air-cooled Beetle engine, although the cylinders and heads were now surrounded by water jackets. The other notable improvement was the addition of a spin-on oil filter. This negated the need for the oil strainer and plate, a simple drain plug being fitted instead, resulting in the oil-change service interval increasing to 5,000 miles (7,500km). The filter is situated at the rear of the engine on the left-hand side and is easily removed using a chain wrench, or one of the many types of oil filter removal tool.

↓ **One of the simplest but most important weekly tasks that should be carried out with all air-cooled engines is to check the engine oil level.**

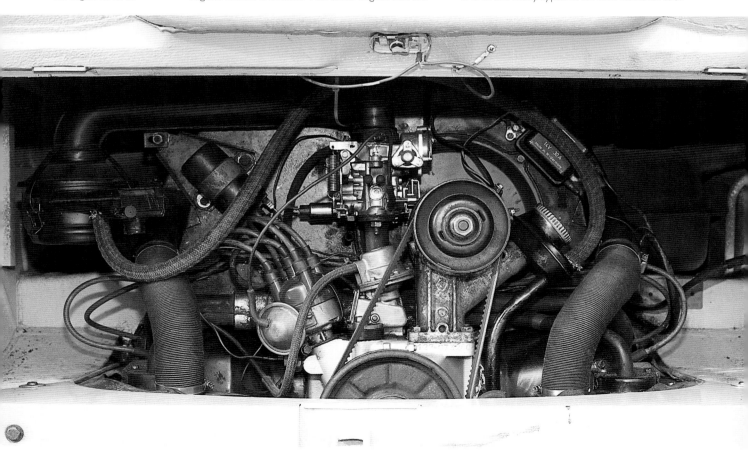

The oil dipstick and oil filler tube are conveniently fitted at the rear of the engine bay just right of centre. Access is gained through a conventional engine lid cover on the Pick-up, or via the flap holding the rear number plate on other models. All third-generation Transporters are fitted with an inspection hatch above the engine, allowing access to the spark plugs and other more involved maintenance procedures.

After checking the oil, the drive belt for the generator, or alternator, should be tested for condition and tension. On Beetle-derived engines the belt drives the fan and is a vital component of the cooling system. To test the tension, press the belt halfway between the pulleys and measure the deflection. This should be between 10 and 12mm for optimum performance. Too tight and the bearings in the generator will suffer, too loose and the belt will slip, leading to insufficient battery charging and a lack of cooling air around the engine. Always check that the generator warning light comes on when you switch on the ignition, and stop immediately if the light comes on while driving. Air-cooled engines will fail very quickly if the fan stops working.

If the belt needs adjustment, the work can be carried out with the simple tools supplied with the vehicle. Using the opposite end of the wheel brace socket, turn the engine so that the cut-out in the rim of the generator pulley lines up with the screw head on the rear of the generator body. It is then possible to hold the pulley by wedging a screwdriver between the cut-out and the screw, thus enabling the large pulley nut to be loosened. To tighten the belt, remove a shim from between the two pulley halves. Reassemble the pulley halves and belt, before placing the shim removed previously under the nut on the outside of the pulley. Tighten the nut while ensuring that the locating lugs on the two pulley halves are correctly aligned.

On air-cooled models it is important to check that all cooling tinware and the foam seal that connects it to the vehicle body in the engine compartment are secure and in good condition. Any gaps may allow hot air from beneath the tinware to be drawn back through the cooling system, reducing its effectiveness.

With the water-cooled third-generation models having the radiator and heater matrix situated at the front of the vehicle and the engine, expansion tank, coolant top-up tank and thermostat located at the rear, major work is best left to the experts, unless you are a competent mechanic. After replacing any component of the cooling system it is quite a

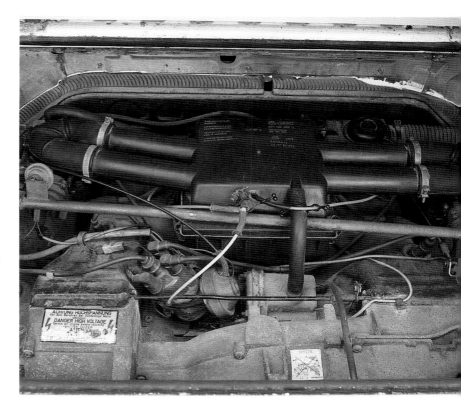

rigmarole to bleed out all the air. However, topping up is easy, as the top-up tank is again located under the number plate flap. Be sure to use the correct VW G12 plus coolant additive (G11 has been superseded), or corrosion of the head studs passing through the water jackets of the cylinders may result.

In addition to the above, the following engine procedures should be carried out as part of the 3,000/5,000-mile service. All wiring, hoses, fuel lines and breather pipes should be checked for condition and replaced if damaged. The fuel filter on petrol engines should be replaced and all fuel hoses should be secured with proper clips. The carburettor(s) should be checked for leaks and adjustment.

The spark plugs on petrol engines should be removed and either cleaned or replaced, and the electrode gap checked, according to the recommended service schedule. The distributor components should be inspected and serviced as necessary, and the ignition timing checked.

On engines without maintenance-free hydraulic tappets, the valve clearances should be checked and adjusted as necessary.

Finally, the exhaust system, including heat exchangers (air-cooled models), should be checked for damage, corrosion and leaks.

**↑ The 2-litre engine carried over from the Bay to the Wedge now featured hydraulic tappets.**

## Suspension and steering

The front suspension on the first two generations of Transporter is achieved through the use of transverse mounted twin torsion bars. These require regular greasing to keep wear to a minimum as does the king pin and link pin assembly fitted to the split screen models. Bay window models are fitted with maintenance-free ball joints to provide the steering action of the stub axle assembly. The upper mounting point for the telescopic damper is located at the top of the end plate holding the two torsion bar tubes to the chassis. The lower shock absorber mount is located on the lower trailing arm. The shock absorbers should be examined regularly for leakage and checked for excessive bounce. Also check the condition of the mounting points.

Early Splitty Transporters used a rubber bump stop mounted between the trailing arms, while later models incorporated the bump stop in the telescopic damper assembly. The worm-and-peg steering box was upgraded to the worm-and-roller type for the 1973 model year. Both types transfer the steering action from the drop arm through a drag link, via a relay lever mounted centrally on the lower torsion

bar tube. The oil level of the steering gear should be checked and topped up if necessary. Track rods fitted with ball joints transfer the steering action from the idler to the stub axles. The protective rubber gaiter surrounding each ball joint should be checked and the whole component replaced if it is split. A regular application of grease is most important to keep wear to a minimum and this should be carried out at 3,000 miles (5,000km) on early models, 6,000 miles (10,000km) on Bay-window Transporters. The front end should be lifted to take the weight off the suspension components before applying grease. There are four rear-facing grease nipples on each end of the torsion bar tubes that should be greased until surplus lubricant appears between the rubber seal and the torsion arm.

The relay lever pivot in the centre of the lower torsion bar should also be greased at this time, two nipples on first-generation models and one on the Bay window. The Splitty also has a nipple on each of the track rod ends and all have two nipples on each of the king and link pin assemblies. The ball-joint type of steering swivel is sealed for life, as are the track rod ends on later models. The front brake drums and wheel bearings should be removed and the hubs packed with grease every 30,000 miles (50,000km). The free-play in the steering should be no more than 15mm in the centre position measured at the steering wheel. All steering components should be checked for play every six months during regular usage. The link pins on the first-generation Transporter should also be checked for excessive play and adjusted if needed. A hydraulic steering damper is connected to the steering and should be periodically checked for fluid leakage. The mounting rubbers and clamps connecting the anti-roll bar to the lower trailing arms do not need regular maintenance, but should be checked periodically for condition.

With the introduction of the third-generation Transporter the front suspension was completely redesigned using upper wishbones, lower track control arms and coil springs over the telescopic dampers. A front anti-roll bar, to help keep body roll to a minimum, and an adjustable radius arm completed the setup. The steering box used previously was discarded in favour of a steering rack, giving a car-like feel to the driving experience. This was especially true of the top-of-the-range Microbus, the Caravelle Carat, a vehicle that had power-assisted steering as part of the standard equipment. Apart from regular checks to the various rubber bushes and ball joints, the suspension and steering is maintenance free. The power steering fluid level requires regular inspection as do the protective gaiters where the track rods exit the steering rack. A sudden drop in fluid level indicates a leak in the system that should be investigated without delay. If the fluid drops below the minimum mark it can froth and damage the power steering pump. The fluid reservoir is situated to the right rear of the engine bay and should be topped up to the maximum-level mark.

To keep tyres in optimum condition the inflation pressures should be checked regularly: too soft and the outer edges will wear prematurely, too hard will wear the centre. Incorrect pressures will affect handling and braking efficiency, as well as having a detrimental effect on fuel economy. VW Transporters are designed as commercial vehicles and should only be fitted with the recommended six-ply tyres. Tread depth is also important, as research shows that less than 2mm can also have a serious effect on the ability to stop in an emergency. This is due to an increased risk of skidding on anything other than a dry surface.

Tyres should also be checked for tracking problems. Excessive wear on the outside shoulders of the tyres indicate toe-in, and wear on the inner edges point to toe-out. Tracking problems can be caused by a number of faults, from worn steering components to hitting a kerb or a pot-hole in the road. Rear wheel tracking is rarely a problem unless an inexperienced person has disconnected the axle tubes or rear wheel bearing housings from the trailing spring plates, without carefully marking the original position first.

The rear suspension of the first-generation models comprises solid torsion bars mounted in a substantial tube forward of the rear axle. Trailing steel spring plates connect the swing axle type drive-shafts to the torsion bars. The final drive ratio is lowered further by geared reduction boxes located at the outer end of the drive shafts. These reduction boxes have their own oil supply that should be checked and topped up every 3,000 miles (5,000km) with SAE 90 Hypoid gear oil. As part of the 30,000 miles (50,000km) service the reduction boxes should be completely drained and refilled with fresh oil. The rubber gaiters where the drive shafts leave the transmission casing need to be checked periodically

for splitting to prevent the loss of oil from the gearbox assembly. Lever arm shock absorbers were fitted prior to March 1953, after which telescopic dampers became the standard fitment. All dampers should be checked for leakage and excessive bounce. To check the condition, push down on each corner of the vehicle and the suspension should return to its original position without bouncing.

With the introduction of the Bay-window model in August 1967, the rear suspension and final drive was completely redesigned. The swing-axles and reduction boxes were replaced by new double-jointed drive shafts with a constant velocity joint at each end. A diagonal beam connecting the wheel bearing housing and trailing spring plate to the chassis kept the camber angle constant, eliminating at a stroke the tuck under of the rear axle previously experienced with the older swing-axle design. The constant velocity joint rubber boots should be inspected for splitting and the six screws holding the joint to the wheel bearing housing and gearbox axle flange should be checked for tightness. The condition of the inner diagonal arm rubber bush should also be checked periodically.

↓ **Reduction box oil level should be inspected regularly and the securing bolts checked for tightness.**

Yet another change of design occurred with the introduction of the third-generation Transporter. The double-jointed drive shafts were retained, but coil springs replaced the torsion bars. The trailing arms that hold the wheel bearing housing are of a wishbone design fastened to brackets on the chassis through rubber bushes. The telescopic dampers are mounted separately from the coil springs, being attached to a bracket at the rear of the trailing arm. The whole assembly is maintenance free, only requiring checks to be made to the drive shaft gaiters, the tightness of the CV joint bolts, and the condition of the rubber bushes in the trailing arms.

## Brakes

The brake fluid level should be checked weekly and any fluid loss investigated immediately as it could lead to a loss of braking efficiency on the road. The fluid is hydroscopic and should be changed every two years, as the absorbed water leads to a loss of stopping power. On first-generation models the reservoir is situated below a panel in the cab floor just behind the brake pedal. Early Bay-window models had the reservoir in the front panel above the top hat cover for the windscreen washer fluid. For 1971 and '72 models the reservoir was moved to behind the driver's seat and in later years under it. The combined brake and clutch fluid reservoir can be found by removing the dashboard cover on third-generation models. Do not overfill the reservoir; about 20mm from the base of the filler neck threads is correct for early models and later models have Max and Min marks on the reservoir.

All Transporters produced before August 1970 were fitted with drum brakes on all four wheels; disc brakes became standard on the front of all subsequent models. Third-generation Transporters have servo assistance and a brake pressure regulator to the rear brakes, and some late models were also fitted with ABS. The Servo can be tested by pumping the brake pedal with the engine switched off, and while keeping your foot pressed hard on the pedal, starting the engine. If all is well the pedal drops slightly when the engine starts. If a fault is suspected with either servo or ABS, take the vehicle to a recognised Volkswagen specialist.

The rear brake shoes and the front shoes on early models can be checked for lining thickness by looking through a hole in the brake drum. The linings are adjusted to the drum by turning the star wheels in a clockwise direction until the brake starts to bind and then back off three clicks. Each wheel has two star wheels. Later models have three holes, protected with rubber bungs in each brake back plate. The lower two holes house the two star wheels for adjusting the shoes to the drum, while the third is for inspecting the thickness of the brake linings. Third-generation Transporters are fitted with self-adjusting drum brakes on the rear axle.

From August 1970, disc brakes were fitted to the front wheels. Pad thickness is easier to check with the front wheels removed. Unless a piston sticks in the brake calliper the disc brakes need very little attention as they are self-adjusting.

The handbrake features a separate cable to each back brake drum on first-generation and Bay models. Third-generation Transporters have a single primary cable from the operating lever to an equaliser bar and then a separate cable to each rear drum. The handbrake should only be adjusted after the shoes have been adjusted to the drums. All models up to 1979 have adjusters on the cable ends adjacent to the handbrake lever. The handbrake is adjusted from beneath the vehicle on third-generation Transporters by means of an adjusting nut on the primary handbrake cable at the equaliser bar.

Periodically, according to the recomended service schedule, the road wheels should be removed and all braking components cleaned and inspected for wear, damage and fluid leakage.

## Clutch and transmission

The clutches on models up to 1979 were operated by a cable running the length of the vehicle. Adjustment is made at the clutch-operating lever on the gearbox and consists of an adjusting nut and lock nut on early models and a shaped wing nut on later vehicles.

The gearbox oil on models up to 1969 should be drained at 30,000 miles (50,000km) and refilled with the correct grade of hypoid oil to the bottom of the filler hole in the side of the casing. Later models only need a gearbox oil change if the transmission has been disassembled. The ATF should also be changed at 30,000 miles on models with automatic transmission, reduced to 18,000 miles (3,000km) if the vehicle is used for towing.

## Miscellaneous

The electrolyte level in the battery should be checked and topped up monthly, unless a 'maintenance-free' battery is fitted. The battery terminals must be cleaned if corrosion is present, and then greased to prevent further build up.

The condition of the windscreen wiper blades should be checked regularly, particularly at the ends where they are prone to splitting.

To keep your Transporter looking good it should be washed frequently. If the water forms large flat patches instead of droplets on the paintwork then a coat of good quality wax polish should be applied. Dull paintwork can be revived with an abrasive liquid polish such as T-cut, which should then be followed up with wax polish to protect the restored paint finish. Special products are available to remove tar spots, insects and tree sap and should be used in preference to harmful substances such as petrol. Apply good quality chrome cleaner to any brightwork, but beware of using it on plastic chromework.

There are literally thousands of products designed to keep the vehicle interior pleasant.

These range from foam upholstery cleaners to products to clean and protect the dashboard. Always use the correct product for the job and follow the manufacturer's instructions to the letter. Plastic bumper mouldings used on later models can be cleaned with dedicated products, although silicon spray works nearly as well. A careful application of heat from a hot-air gun also works to restore faded bumper trim, but care must be taken to prevent over doing it, as it is possible to smooth out the grain pattern if too much heat is applied.

A thorough inspection of the bodywork and chassis should be carried out periodically, and any damage or corrosion dealt with appropriately. Small paint scratches can often be polished out or touched up whereas rust in panels or seams should receive remedial attention to prevent, or at least delay, expensive repairs in the future. The chassis and underside should be coated with one of the many products available to protect against water, stone-chips and corrosion. In addition, check that all drainage holes at the bottom of doors and sills are clear and consider having enclosed panel sections injected with a proprietary corrosion inhibitor.

↑ **A careful application of heat from a hot air gun also works to restore faded bumper trim.**

# CHAPTER 10
# GETTING THE MOST OUT OF YOUR TRANSPORTER

Whichever way you look at it, Volkswagen's first-generation Transporter is grossly underpowered for today's traffic conditions. With just 25bhp available for the earliest vehicles, unless originality for concours is the aim, the majority of owners look for an engine with more power. The first choice for many is the twin-port 1,600cc engine fitted as standard in the second-generation Transporter, the Bay. With an immediate increase in power to 50bhp and looking, at first glance, similar to the original unit, the advantages are obvious.

The 1,600cc engine is also highly tuneable with kits available to increase the capacity from the original 1,584cc all the way up to 2 litres and beyond. Above 1,641cc the crankcase and the cylinder heads require machining to accept the outer diameter of the larger cylinder barrels. Forged pistons rather than cast are a stronger option for the larger capacity engines. Longer stroke crankshafts, known as 'stroker crankshafts' are required to achieve the highest capacities.

Due to the increase in power and torque, stroker crankshafts are usually machined to accept eight dowels to hold the flywheel in place. The crankcase also requires machining to allow clearance for the longer throw of the stroker crankshaft and connecting rods. The larger capacity engines also need cylinder heads fitted with bigger valves to improve breathing and a high lift camshaft to extract the maximum power. Topped with twin Weber or Dell'Orto carburettors considerably more power can be achieved. The main disadvantage of the larger engines is the inevitable increase in oil temperature, which needs taming with a higher capacity oil pump, full-flow oil filter and, where possible, an external oil cooler.

In the interests of safety, urgent attention to beef up the brakes and suspension should also be considered. However, disc brake conversions along with high-performance shock absorbers and suspension components are now readily available for Split-screen models. Advantages of the standard 1,600cc engine include a wider, high capacity cooling fan and a larger oil cooler, known as a dog-leg cooler, mounted in a separate compartment in front of the fan housing. This allows more cooling air to reach the allegedly hotter No. 3 cylinder.

There may be a clearance problem between the original gearbox bell housing and the flywheel assembly of a 12-volt engine, which may require remedial work. Be aware that where the flywheel meets the crankshaft there are detail differences between 6-volt and 12-volt engines; the 6-volt crankshaft is stepped at the flywheel end and requires a different combination of gaskets. The flywheel starter rings are also different with the 6-volt engine having 109 teeth, whereas its 12-volt counterpart has 130 teeth. Some late 6-volt engines also have a flywheel with 130 teeth. This may necessitate some clearance work to be carried out on the bell housing before fitting a 12-volt engine to a vehicle originally supplied with a 6-volt unit.

The original clutch made for a Bay-window Transporter is either 200mm or 215mm depending on year and may not clear the inside of the bell housing. If also changing to 12-volt electrics, the starter motor bush housed in the bell housing will have to be replaced. This is due to the 6-volt and 12-volt starter motor shafts being of different diameters. This may necessitate having a starter bush specially made to accept the 12-volt shaft. Most owners get away with using the 6-volt starter and running 12 volt through it to start the vehicle. However, care must be taken not to run the starter too long as there is a danger of it burning out. Front and rear tin-ware panels and cylinder shrouds for a 1303S Beetle will also be required along with an alternator and stand from a 1,600cc Bay Transporter or late-model Beetle. The wiring connected to the original voltage regulator will require adapting, to connect up with the built-in regulator integral with the alternator brushes.

← More powerful engines can be fitted to all Transporters. In Splitties and Bays, most often larger air-cooled engines are used, whilst for a Wedge there are plenty of water-cooled petrol and diesel options, some not even from the Volkswagen stable. With the original engine out, it is literally a case of working with a blank canvas.

## 1700, 1800 and 2-litre engines in a Bay

From August 1971, the engine originally designed to power Volkswagen's largest saloon, the VW 411 or Type 4, became an option for most markets and the standard unit in the USA. To accommodate this larger unit the engine bay increased in both width and length and the once-bolted-in rear panel was now welded in place, making engine removal more difficult. Known as the pancake or suitcase engine due to the cooling fan being fitted to the rear of the crankshaft, this is a much stronger unit and a very desirable replacement for the ubiquitous Type 1 or Beetle-based 1,600cc engine or even a 1,300cc unit if the vehicle originated from Italy.

It is usual to find twin carburettors on the Type 4 style engines, but in March 1974 a fuel-injection system was introduced to meet ever more stringent exhaust emission laws in California. In August 1974, this was rolled out over the entire North American continent, although Europe doggedly stuck to using twin carburettors to the end of Bay-window production.

The original 1,700cc engine produced 66bhp.

However, there are infinite varieties of these units produced for different market requirements throughout the world that are impossible to list in this volume. Generally those produced specifically for the Type 2 have a lower compression ratio and are less powerful than the units produced for the VW 411, 412 and the VW-Porsche 914-4. The various options are further complicated by certain models being equipped with an electronic fuel injection system. The Type 2 Bay-window model built for the USA market received the 66bhp, twin-carburettor engine when first introduced in August 1971. This increased to 68bhp when the engine capacity was enlarged to 1,800cc in November 1973. The fuel-injected 1,800cc unit produced 70bhp as did all versions of the 2-litre engine, albeit, with a considerable increase in torque from the larger unit. Some of the engines sourced from a VW 411LE or 412LE are also fitted with electronic fuel injection.

Fitting these stronger engines to a Bay originally supplied with the Type 1-based 1600 unit is a fairly straightforward procedure, providing all ancillaries and tin-ware belonging to the Type 4-style unit are present. The rear engine mounting bar, engine

↓ **The picture illustrates the go-faster practice of fitting a 1600 twin-port engine to a Splitty.**

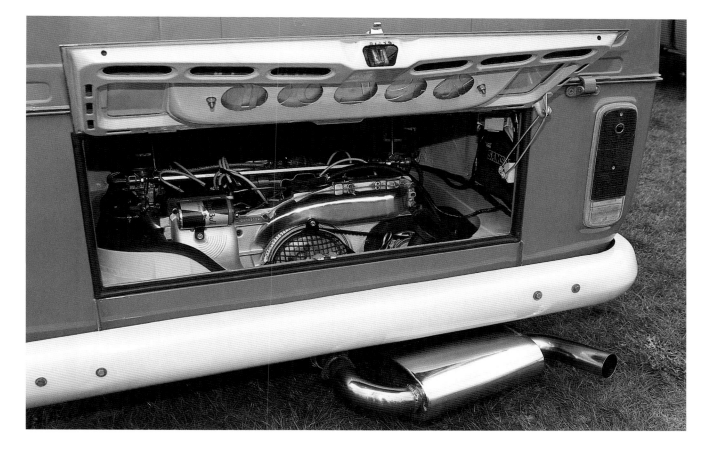

mounts and brackets for the larger engine, plus the exhaust system and heat exchangers, should also be used as they are of a completely different design to the 1600 items. The twin-carburettor setup will also require the air cleaner and associated pipe-work to replace those made for the 1,600cc engine. The accelerator cable is located in a slightly different position on vehicles originally fitted with Type 4 engines, but this is easily modified when fitting this unit to a Transporter previously fitted with the 1,600cc unit. The throttle cable may need to be changed depending on the year of the recipient vehicle.

Post 1975 a larger diameter clutch and a different starter motor will also be required. Prior to August 1971, the tin-ware of the 1,600cc engine was surrounded by a double flat seal, after which a continuous foam seal was used necessitating the use of flat-edged tin-ware. Fitting the Type 4 engine to these earlier models necessitates using a plastic or glass-fibre fan housing that utilises the fan and alternator from a Porsche 911 and is available from custom parts suppliers. The result is a considerably smaller engine unit making it possible to fit it into a Split-screen or early Bay Transporter. It is still

essential when using this conversion to seal the engine bay to prevent hot air, exhaust fumes and heat being drawn into the cooling fan. The gearbox input shaft will also need to be replaced, using the shaft from a bus fitted with a Type 4 engine.

The generator fitted to early 1600 engines uses an external voltage regulator mounted on the right-hand bulkhead forward of the engine. When fitting a Type 4 unit, this will need to be replaced by an external voltage regulator suited to the alternator and also mounted on the bulkhead. If fitting to a later Bay supplied originally with a 1,600cc engine and using an alternator with an integral regulator, a wiring loom will be needed to connect to the bulkhead mounted regulator. Type 4-style engines also require an electric motor and pipe assembly connected to the heat exchanges to provide warm air to the vehicle interior.

Considerably more power can be achieved if larger capacity pistons and barrels are used, along with a long throw stroker crankshaft and cylinder heads fitted with bigger valves. Power benefits can also be achieved by using a high-lift camshaft in conjunction with the above modifications.

↑ Although this may have been the original engine, a late 1600 Bay will readily accept the beefier Type 4-style power unit.

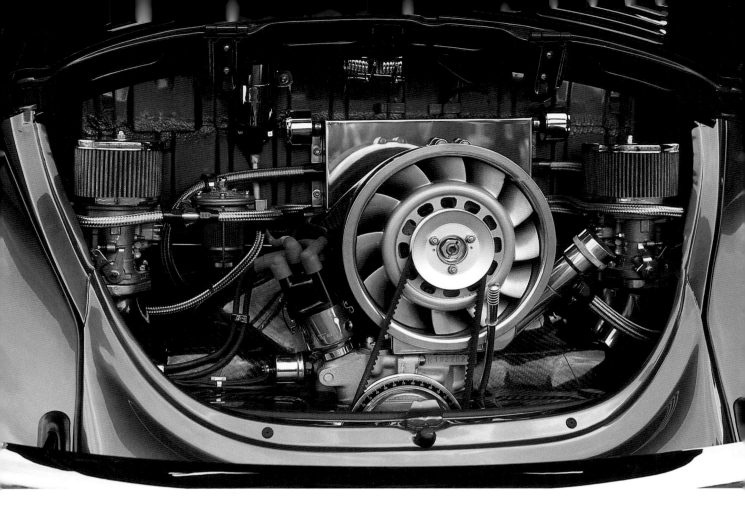

↑ **This Porsche 911-style fan and housing, pictured here on a Type 1 engine fitted to a Beetle, is also available for Type 4 engines. This is the best option when fitting such an engine to a Splitty, or an early Bay.**

The engine breathing can be further improved by fitting suitable Weber or Dell'Orto carburettors on manifolds designed for these engines.

## Audi 80 GT engine in a Type 25

A worthwhile conversion to replace the underpowered diesel unit fitted to Type 25 models is to opt for one of the powerful four-cylinder petrol units from the VW/Audi stable, in this case from an Audi GT from the late 1980s. Engines from 8v Golf GTIs or 16v KR series engines from Golf GTIs, Corrados and Passats also make good donor units.

Due to the height of some of the ancillary components this conversion is easiest when performed on the Type 25 Pick-up. This is because the load platform and overhead engine covers are positioned higher in a Pick-up than models based on the Delivery Van or Kombi. The metering head for the K-Jetronic-fuel injection system will need to be relocated within the engine compartment when this conversion is performed on a Delivery van or Kombi.

This conversion, although possible, is not so worthwhile on models fitted with the water-cooled boxer engine as a 112bhp version of the flat four is already available as an option. The diesel models also have the hoses leading to the front-mounted radiator, in the correct position for any of the in-line four-cylinder petrol units. Some modification would be required to align the pipe work on models previously powered by a water-boxer engine.

As the engine is inclined steeply to the left to allow height clearance, the sump and oil pick-up pipe from the Type 25 1,600cc diesel unit will need to be transferred to the petrol donor engine. A small amount of modification to the engine compartment bodywork on the nearside will also be needed to provide enough clearance for the inlet manifold.

If the vehicle receiving the donor engine happens to be a syncro model, the original fuel tank can be used. All other models will require a brand-new fuel tank with a larger fuel outlet pipe brazed or soldered in at its lowest point. On no account try to do this to the existing tank as it is illegal and highly dangerous due to a very real risk of an explosion.

The multi-plug previously used for the glow plug relay that is situated to the left in the front of the engine compartment, can be rewired to power the fuel pump relay for the Bosch K-Jetronic fuel-injection system.

Modifications to the exhaust system are limited to fitting a short length of flexible tubing between the manifold and the intermediate pipe. The original intermediate pipe and silencer box from the 1,600cc diesel engine can be reused.

## Diesel options

If the frugal fuel consumption of a diesel engine is desired one of the later 1.9-litre turbo-diesel units from a Golf, Passat or an Audi can be used. Again the sump and oil pick-up tube from the Type 25 diesel engine will need to be transferred to the donor engine and the exhaust will have to be modified in a similar way to that described above.

South African-built Type 25s made after European production ceased were fitted with the five-cylinder, fuel-injected unit as used by Audi in the 1980s.

↑ **The Audi 80 GT engine is a recommended and easily achieved option for enthusiasts wishing to upgrade the power of their water-cooled Wedge.**

↓ **This Audi V6 TDI engine has been successfully wedged into a third-generation Transporter, but would not normally be regarded as a suitable option for anyone other than a skilled mechanic. A diesel engine from a Golf would fit more easily although some modification is necessary.**

# CHAPTER 11
# A MATTER OF PERSONAL TASTE

The ways to customise a Volkswagen Transporter are many and varied. There's the archetypal Hippie Bus, often frayed at the edges, frequently lowered and invariably painted with either large flower motifs over the original body colour, or liberally daubed with hand applied graphics over much of the panel-work. More often than not the examples seen today are Bay-window campers, but a few Split-screen examples from the numerous ones created when the first-generation Transporter was just an old people-carrier still exist.

These days, there are even a few Wedges falling into this category, although most that now sport flower-power designs were not in the best of condition previously. Look inside and you are likely to find a miniature skeleton or troll hanging from the mirror, the inner panels, door cards and even the ceiling covered with long mohair carpet, and the seats, curtains and scatter cushions in floral or patterned cloth. You may also find the obligatory didgeridoo mounted on brackets forward of the rear seat. While the above is clearly intended to convey the archetypal image of such vehicles, nevertheless the picture painted is pertinent. The same style of Transporter can often be found near popular surfing beaches with surf boards on the roof rack and music blaring from the sound system.

Originating in the United States and the sunshine state of California, both Cal-look and Resto Cal-look are popular choices for the avid custom concours entrant. They are always lowered, often too low, 'in the weeds' or 'slammed' as their exponents proclaim, and are usually immaculately painted in non-standard, often garish colours. The Cal-look vehicles usually have any standard issue, bright trim removed whereas Resto Cal-look owners leave what little there is in place. Sometimes even the door handles are removed in the interest of smoothing out the lines of the body. In such instances the doors are opened remotely using solenoid-operated door locks. Aftermarket wheels are frequently fitted; with

EMPI five-spoke or Porsche-style Fuch replica wheels being amongst the most popular choices.

In strict contrast to the bodywork the engine compartment is often a mass of bright work, ranging from billet aluminium pulleys, marked out in degrees of crankshaft rotation, to chrome-plated fan housings and tin-ware. Alternatively, the tin-ware is painted in the body colour or a complementary hue, in fact any finish except the original Satin Black. Electrical components such as the generator and the distributor body are regularly chrome plated, while the distributor cap can be a custom-made transparent plastic item in a colour to match the tin-ware. With a myriad of custom dress-up parts readily available from specialists the possibilities are endless. The standard exhaust system is more often than not replaced with one of the various designs of extractor system available off the shelf from custom parts suppliers.

The interiors of Cal-look Transporters are typically of a bespoke design and are usually finished to a high standard either by their owners or by one of the skilled coach trimmers specialising in these vehicles. All this is invariably accompanied by a state-of-the-art ICE system with enormous speakers, pushing out enough power to fill The Royal Albert Hall.

The most recent trend is the phenomenon of the Rat-look Transporter. These range from tired examples being brought back into use, without any attempt to restore rusty or damaged bodywork, to a reasonably tidy vehicle being deliberately aged and given a dull finish. A good number of this latter category of vehicle have been imported from the dry and sunny areas of the United States or Australia, where the effects of the intense sunlight has already virtually removed or at least bleached most of the paint. To preserve these vehicles in their 'as-found' state they are either sprayed with clear lacquer or coated with Anchor Wax to prevent further deterioration. (Unfortunately, Anchor Wax is not a permanent solution to bodywork preservation,

**← Here's the opportunity to do what you like, either spending a fortune or scrabbling around in a scrap yard! The owner of this early Bay has spent his money on a spoiler, a pair of auxiliary driving lights and a pair of fog lamps mounted on the bumper. He's also indulged his passion for badges having first fitted quadruple badge bars. Note also the lorry style mirrors, the chromed wiper arms, and the grille embellisher. Maybe not to everyone's taste, but there's no reason why a future owner couldn't return this Transporter to its original specification.**

→ Although this delicately painted flower epitomises the flower-power era, in this instance it has been applied in much more recent times in true retro style.

↓ This simple summery interpretation of camping days with blue waves and golden sands caught the eye some years ago now.

requiring annual application to carry out the task required of it.)

An additional Rat-look ruse is to sign-write a Panel van with a company name in a style and typeface to match the vehicle's era of manufacture, and then employ the various aging techniques required, such as removing small parts of the graphics, and rubbing sections through to the primer, to achieve the desired look. Some owners of Panel vans have been lucky enough to find graphics and company names dating back to the 1950s and 1960s when removing a more recently applied coat of paint.

Mechanically, Rat-look Transporters must at least be capable of gaining a roadworthiness certificate and often have had a lot of attention lavished on the underside. Repairs to any damage on the chassis rails and outriggers before thorough protection with paint and under-body preparations can often be found. In line with recent trends, Rat-look vehicles are often lowered and in extreme cases have narrowed front beams to allow the front wheels to turn without rubbing on the cab step area. Somewhat curiously, they are then often fitted with modern alloy wheels, wider tyres and a shiny extractor exhaust system.

Finally, there's the individual approach, where the owner or customising workshop creates a completely unique vehicle, often bristling with accessories. The bodywork may include a chopped-down roof, front air-dam spoiler, or smoothed off front, completely removing the fixing points for the badge in the case of the first two generations of Transporter. A recent trend has been to change the front fresh-air ventilation grille on a Bay-window model, for one with cut-out graphics chosen by the owner. A popular area for individuality is the lighting arrangement, where maybe a twin-headlight system finds its way on to the front of a Bay or Ford Cortina MkI rear-lights (or similar) are grafted on to the rear,

↑ **Hand-applied graphics over much of the panel-work.**

to name some extreme examples. An immaculately prepared paint finish with air-brushed graphics is another popular individualistic choice to attract the attention of the custom Concours judge.

The mechanical possibilities are endless; some customised models might have been fitted with a Subaru Impreza engine developing around 145bhp, while it is not beyond the realms of impossibility to shoehorn the unit from a Porsche 911 into the back of a Transporter. Stopping ability is easily up-rated with Porsche 944 disc brakes being available in a kit to convert the drum brakes of a Split-screen or early Bay, while rear disc brake kits are readily available for all models. A kit is also available to allow Porsche Boxster discs and callipers to be fitted to a third-generation Transporter. Most Porsche brake kits require 15in or larger wheels to allow sufficient clearance for the beefier callipers.

It is currently fashionable to lower the suspension on Volkswagen Transporters which, if done properly, can improve the handling and body roll characteristics considerably. Although not so noticeable on torsion bar-equipped Transporters, the use of beam-mounted ride-height adjusters alters the factory-designed steering geometry and can cause

the ride to become very harsh, with bump steer and other handling problems becoming a real possibility. There are components available to help solve these problems but they may not cure them altogether. Due to such considerations, using the beam-mounted ride-height adjuster method described below can only be recommended for either aesthetic reasons, or budget constraints.

Adjusters may also be employed to fine-tune the ride height when used in combination with dropped spindles that allow a fixed drop of 2½in (65mm). These adjusters are usually referred to as 'Sway-Aways' and involve cutting a piece from each of the two front beams and welding in a section with an adjustable centre torsion bar leaf anchor. When fitted, these adjusters allow the ride height to be altered at will.

This method of lowering is often coupled to a procedure that narrows the front beam, allowing much wider wheels and tyres to be fitted. However, care must be taken as wider tyres can foul the front step area of a lowered vehicle. The narrowing procedure also involves cutting sections out of each side of the beam, welding narrow end plates to the torsion beam tubes, shortening the torsion bar leaves and re-drilling dimples for the torsion arm locating bolts. Such a process requires a high level of welding and engineering skill, as the life of the driver and occupants of a vehicle so treated depends on the integrity of the finished beam. The track rods also require shortening for use with narrowed beams. Pre-lowered and narrowed front beams are available from some specialist custom parts suppliers. Additionally, shorter shock absorbers will be required using this lowering method.

A much better, but more expensive, way to lower the front of Split-screen and Bay-window Transporters is to fit drop spindles. These rebuilt stub axles give a 2½in drop to the ride height without any of the hassle caused by altering the steering geometry. Drop spindles are available with the provision to convert the drum brake of Splitty and early Bays to the later standard disc brake setup, or to upgrade to Porsche 944, four-pot calipers. A dual-circuit master cylinder, as used on disc brake-equipped Bay-window models, must be used with these brake upgrades. This method of lowering can also be combined with a narrowed front beam to allow sufficient clearance for the wheels and tyres under the front step area. Lowering the third-generation Transporter is simply a matter of changing the coil springs and dampers for a set designed to reduce the ride height by 40mm.

Hydraulic suspension units are another favoured option of the custom brigade. These allow the ride height to be adjusted at will from ultra low for cruising around shows to a more reasonable height for normal driving on the road.

Over the years, many an aftermarket spoiler has been fitted to all generations of Transporter. These are usually the air-dam type fixed to the front of the vehicle for aesthetic reasons, although the makers claim they help to stabilise the front when driving in a cross-wind. Customised third-generation Transporters often feature full body kits, consisting of an extended front bumper to form a spoiler, matching rear bumper, and side skirts.

One of the most worthwhile additions to a Transporter converted for use as a camper is the elevating roof as these allow most adults to stand upright in the rear accommodation area of the vehicle. Various companies can supply and fit elevating roofs and in Great Britain these include the ones outlined below.

O'Connors Campers based in Okehampton, Devon supply and fit a roof manufactured in Germany similar in design to the one originally produced by Westfalia. This is a three-quarter front-lifting elevating roof, with canvas sides, and features zipped front and side windows. Each kit comprises all the fixtures and fittings required, including a support frame and cross member, while the addition of a 6ft × 4ft roof-mounted double bed platform comes as a welcome bonus. These roofs can be fitted to Bay-window and later models of Transporter including the T4 and T5, plus the latest Bays still being manufactured in Brazil. The only additional cost is for the 50mm thick foam for the bed, and the upholstery covering, as this part of the operation is farmed out to a local expert. O'Connors Campers is also developing a turret style pop-top elevating roof for Split-screen models again based on the original Westfalia design.

The original Dormobile Company ceased trading many years ago now, but the name has recently reappeared, and the new company now based at Romsey, Hampshire, is again making the traditional side-opening Dormobile roof kits for Split-screen and Bay-window models as well as other vehicles. Improvements over the original product include opening polycarbonate windows in place of the fragile, fixed acrylic roof lights, and a roof lining to make the interior more cosy. If converting a vehicle

↓ **Cal-look vehicles are denuded of trim. This example has a smoothed front panel, eliminating the fresh air intake grille.**

→ This is a fine example of the Retro-Cal style.

↓ Chromed, painted and polished, in the Custom Concours scene there are points to be amassed for work of this standard.

→ A Rat-look Bay featuring many recent trends, including a very low stance and a narrowed front beam.

→ → A mixture of styles, Rat-look paint finish with shiny accessories and lowered suspension.

↑ Rat-look fans delight in presenting genuine old graphics found on a vehicle, or conversely deliberately aging 21st century lettering for that all-important period look.

← This Rat-look Splitty is regularly treated with vegetable oil to preserve its distinctive look.

↑ The roof section of this Wedge Panel van has been given the chop treatment, transforming the look of the vehicle at a relatively low cost.

↓ This Bay has undergone a typical Camper conversion with a front-mounted spare wheel and a Sheldon high-top roof.

previously fitted with a Devon roof, additional welding and paint spraying will be required at extra cost. The company claims that from the outside, the new Dormobile roof is virtually indistinguishable from the original item. The prices asked for all of the above roofs start at around a quarter of the cost of a good-quality Bay-window Camper.

An owner of a Bay-window Devon Camper suffering from a leaky pop-top can now buy a glass-fibre roof cap from Just Kampers, based at Odiham, Hampshire. The roof cap is glue bonded on to the original Devon roof, and the kit contains everything needed to finish the job, all for the price of a set of five tyres.

Failing all of the above an owner might scrap the existing elevating roof and fit a 'rag-top' sunroof such as that supplied by Paris Beetles, based in Essex. Paris Beetles does not offer a fitting service, and so the options are to either tackle the project at home, or to take the sunroof to a local specialist. The Riviera Roof Company in Gravesend, Kent offers a sliding fibre-glass sunroof as well as a full-length roof replacement, again in fibre-glass, for those owners wanting to revert to the 'tin-top' look.

← Today this customised **Splitty** would be frowned on by the Concours perfectionist. The cooling slots at the rear are vertical and the headlights are upright and recessed into the front panel.

↓ A good example of the lowered and narrowed front beam treatment so beloved by many a custom fan.

→ The ventilation grille of this **Bay** has been replaced with a neatly executed and personalised laser-cut version.

↓ Roo-bars were often fitted to the earlier generations of Transporters used in the Australian outback. (Note that the vehicle pictured is an **Australian Campmobile** and the kangaroo bars were part of the original conversion package.)

← ↓ The Devon-based firm **O'Connors Campers** fit top quality **Westfalia**-style elevating roofs, complete with double bed. The vehicle shown also sports an elegant, colour-coded spare wheel cover, alloy wheels, chrome bumpers and a side step below the sliding door.

# CHAPTER 12
# AFTER THE THIRD-GENERATION

For Volkswagen the story of the Transporter certainly did not end when production of the third-generation model ceased. In anticipation of the launch of the T4, as the fourth-generation model was officially known, the Hanover plant was restructured to accommodate the automated installation of axles, engines and gearboxes, banishing for ever the older method of overhead work. In 1989, the last full year of Wedge production, 147,539 Transporters were built. In 1991, the first full year of T4 production there was a 10,000-unit drop to 137,682, but the following year this number had more than bounced back to 167,830 vehicles. Throughout the T4's 12-year production run, sales hovered in this kind of region, the year 2000 seeing 162,699 units manufactured, but 1993 bearing witness to just 129,779 new vehicles.

Until recently there was no indication that the enthusiast market favoured the T4, but as even later water-cooled Wedge prices have started to escalate, and either age or the introduction of the T5 has started to soften the T4 market in the all-important camper field, there are murmurings at least, of an infant following for the vehicle. One day this may see a revival in the model's fortunes, as has been the case with all its predecessors.

If the abandonment of air-cooling just a few years into production of the third-generation Transporter was declared to be at best radical, or at worst heresy, the last vestiges of Volkswagen's Transporter heritage were eradicated with the launch of the T4. Inevitably, those charged with promoting the new model had a great deal to say.

'Now comes the new Transporter, a brand-new vehicle developed at enormous cost to take van owners into the next century. Much thought has gone into every aspect of its design. From the front engine with front-wheel drive, to the low flat load floor and wide opening rear doors. From the moulded dashboard and door panels, to the independent suspension front and rear. From

the aerodynamic shape, to the extensive anti-corrosion treatment. But the story doesn't end with a new van, because the Transporter is now a complete range of vehicles. For the first time in this category Volkswagen will be supplying chassis cabs ... Two wheelbases, four engines, three payloads and a variety of body styles can all be added to Volkswagen's enviable reputation for reliability and economy to make the new Transporter a real success.'

Volkswagen decided that it was timely to abandon the superior traction, closer to constant weight distribution regardless of load, and more or less rectangular space availability, associated with a rear-engine, rear-wheel-drive vehicle in favour of a by now highly conventional front engine and front-wheel-drive arrangement. The advantages of this kind of set-up come in the form of superior handling in most people's eyes, and more room at the rear, thanks to the disappearance of the hefty bump over the engine. Conversely, as the space over the engine could not be used in the T4, requiring both the driver and front-seat passengers to be positioned further back in the vehicle, the load space in the short-wheelbase version of the T4 was less than in the third-generation model. However, as the cab was further back and there was nothing over the engine, it was possible to rake both the engine lid and windscreen, achieving a more streamlined front that helped the vehicle aerodynamically, leading to a healthy drag coefficient of 0.37.

At both the front and rear, the suspension was described as compact, and in the case of the former, made use of double wishbones and torsion bars, together with short shock absorbers that negated the need to project into the cab's foot-well area. At the rear diagonal trailing arms and coil springs were utilised, while the shock absorbers were mounted below the load floor.

At launch, four new transversely mounted engines were available, servicing being made easier by the

← The fourth- and fifth-generation Transporters will undoubtedly become classics as the years pass by. Indeed, there are already signs that fourth-generation models, especially in Camper guise, are starting to appreciate in value. Once underpowered compared to its contemporaries, thanks to the diesel revolution and VW's 'Pumpe Düse' technology the latest Transporters offer owners considerable power, excellent fuel economy and luxuries unheard of 20 years ago.

commercial vehicles within the range. In Germany, the T4 passenger-carrying options came under the global heading of Multivan. In Britain however, this was deemed inappropriate and the Wedge Caravelle designation was adopted. Inevitably, both trim and engine specifications developed over the years.

Although more vehicles than the Transporter have represented Volkswagen's commercial range for many years, without doubt it is this vehicle that remains the anchor by which this division of the business is judged. Volkswagen was therefore no doubt delighted by the Commercial Vehicles division result in 2006, when some 442,000 Caddys, Crafters (and LTs), plus Transporters were sold, representing a 10 per cent increase on the previous year and another all-time best. In the UK, the T5 Transporter accounted for over half of the total commercial sales with 13,817 vehicles delivered during the year.

The T5 made its debut for the 2003 model year and, by the time it filtered its way through to the UK in Transporter form, was available with four diesel engines, each of which featured TDI 'Pumpe Düse' (PD) technology. After many years of quoting performance in brake-horsepower, at least in Britain and America, metrification had now made its mark, with PS or Pferdestärke being used. Fortunately, the difference is relatively insignificant, in that for example 75PS equates to 73.9bhp. The range consists of a 1,896cc four-cylinder engine, developing 85PS at 3,500rpm, and producing 200Nm maximum torque at 2,000rpm, and a second engine of the same capacity and number of cylinders that develops 104PS at 3,500rpm and maximum torque of 250Nm at 2,000rpm.

Dependent on which vehicle the respective engines are linked to, top speeds of around 91mph (146kph) and a 0–62mph (0–100kph) figure of 23.6 seconds are applicable to the 85PS engine, and 99mph (159kph) and 18.4 seconds to the 104PS. Both are mated to a five-speed gearbox. Two five-cylinder units with six-speed gearboxes top the range. Both have a cubic capacity of 2,460cc, the less powerful one developing 130PS at 3,500rpm and a maximum of 340Nm of torque at 2,000rpm, the other pumping out 174PS at 3,500rpm, with maximum torque of 400Nm occurring again at 2,000rpm. Top speeds with a manual gearbox are 104mph (167kph) and 117mph (188kph) respectively, and 0–62 performance 15.3 seconds and 12.2 seconds accordingly.

↑ **Like its predecessors, the T4 proved popular with the various firms in the business of manufacturing campers. The example shown is the work of Reimo, one of several to receive official approval by Volkswagen Motorhomes in Britain.**

simple expedient of a moveable radiator. A five-speed box was standard across the range, while the four-wheel-drive offerings made use of Volkswagen's syncro system with its viscous coupling providing the necessary drive to the rear wheels. The petrol engines consisted of a 1.8-litre carburettor version that developed 67bhp at 4,000rpm, with maximum torque of 149Nm at 2,200rpm, and a 2.0-litre fuel-injected unit that developed 84bhp at 4,300rpm and maximum torque of 159Nm at 2,200rpm. (This engine was also available with a power-sapping catalytic converter.)

The diesel options consisted of a 1.9-litre unit offering 61bhp at 3,700rpm, with maximum torque of 127Nm being developed between 1,700rpm and 2,500rpm. The larger, 2.4-litre diesel engine was the only five-cylinder option and developed 78bhp at 3,700rpm and 164Nm of torque between 1,800rpm and 2,200rpm.

Finally, in this whistle-stop sketch of the T4, the short-wheelbase version measured 4,879mm (188½in) in length, 1,840mm (72.4in) in width, and 1,910mm (75.2in) in height, making it some 274mm longer than its predecessor, while widths and heights were more or less the same. Generally, the name Transporter was intended to be applied to the

Three of the diesel options are available in the passenger-carrying vehicles, still referred to as the Caravelle in the UK. The 85PS option isn't available, while the 130PS engine can also be specified with a six-speed automatic gearbox with Tiptronic automatic transmission. The 174PS model is also available in automatic transmission mode, but can also be coupled to the 4MOTION four-wheel-drive system and a manual box. In recognition that some customers might still prefer to purchase a petrol-fuelled T5, what is described as a state-of-the-art, 235PS, V6 engine, producing 315Nm maximum torque, and only available with a six-speed automatic gearbox with Tiptronic, has been added.

As will undoubtedly have been suspected, the T5 in short-wheelbase guise is a bigger vehicle than its predecessor, measuring 4,890mm (192in) in length, (4,879mm T4) 1,904mm (75in) in width, (1,840mm T4), and 1,969mm (77in) in height with a low roof (1,910mm T4).

To say that the Transporter range is extensive is no exaggeration. Apart from the four engine options, two wheelbases are on offer, plus three roof heights, and four gross vehicle weights that range from 2.6t to 3.2t, designated accordingly as the T26, T28, T30, and T32. Inevitably not every gross weight can be matched to all roof heights, but nevertheless, the options are near mind boggling! The Panel van, for example, is available in all gross weights as a 3,000mm (118in) short-wheelbase vehicle and in all but T26 guise with a medium roof. With a long wheelbase, there are three roof options for the Panel van, varying from low, to medium, and finally high roof, all of which were available as either a T30 or T32.

The Kombi, as air-cooled owners would have known it, is no more, for in T5 guise, as it had been in the later years of the T4, 'Kombi' has come to mean two rows of seats and windows for the rear-seat occupants, matched to a Panel van-like rear area with metal sides. Kombis are offered in T30 and T32 form, as is a new entrant in the field, at least as far as traditional designations were concerned. The Window van is described as 'Volkswagen's heavy-duty answer to passenger carrying', with seating for up to nine and a hardwearing rubber floor area. Windows can be deleted 'for specialist passenger carrying or conversion'.

Finally, at launch in the Transporter range were the 'Chassis and double cab', both of which

were centred around the long-wheelbase and the T30 option.

With the Caravelle displaying so many features as standard, of which a car owner of a few years ago would have been envious, and, at long last, a genuine Volkswagen Camper and a very luxurious one at that, together with a catalogue of driving/safety/mechanical features fitted to all models, the current T5 bears little resemblance to its ancestor, the first-generation Transporter. However, with nearly 60 years between the launch of the first and the latest incarnation of the Transporter, perhaps that is not as incredible as it may at first sound.

The T5's features include ABS (anti-lock brake system), EDL (electronic differential lock) and TCS (traction control system), plus EBC (engine braking control) and, as an option on the Kombi and above, ESP (electronic stabilisation programme), a feature that was standard on the Caravelle. Again at launch for the Caravelle the list of luxury features was impressive and included air-conditioning with manual adjustment, aluminium or burr wood inserts in the door and side panel trim, Climatronic air-conditioning, electric windows, high-grade sound systems with CD changer with remote control and eight speakers, central locking, and tinted windows.

The ever-swelling numbers of the first, second and third
generation related clubs, the proliferation of traders selling new
and second-hand parts, and the incredible attraction of events
where the Transporter is dominant, attests to its unending
popularity. For all concerned, long may it continue!

# CLUBS, TRADERS AND TRANSPORTER SHOWS

Thanks to the ever-increasing popularity of the Transporter in its first three guises, and the inevitability of Volkswagen dealers having moved on from such elderly machinery, a thriving industry of parts and panel suppliers, camper accessory companies and vehicle traders exists. Additionally, there are a number of clubs that offer support, advice, camaraderie, and more, to both owners and would-be purchasers. One of the best ways of becoming involved with the Transporter scene is to attend one or more of the shows held each year for Transporters, or where there is a large presence of the type.

The list below is not intended to be exhaustive and doesn't imply recommendation, but merely recognises some of the better-known names in the world of the Volkswagen Transporter.

## CLUBS

The Split Screen Van Club
www.ssvc.org.uk
E-mail: membership@ssvc.org.uk

Type 2 Owners Club
01527 872194
www.vwt2oc.org

Club 80–90 – Wedge-owners' club
www.club80-90.co.uk

## TRADE

Calypso Campers – interiors and sales
www.calypsocampers.co.uk
01722 744777

Cool Air – parts
www.coolairvw.co.uk
01322 335050

Creative Engineering – IRS kits,
narrowed beams, custom kits
www.creativeengineering.com
01258 863600

Danbury Motor Caravans – brand new
Brazilian built Bay Transporters
www.danburymotorcaravans.com
0870 1202 356

Dormobile – elevating roofs and restoration
parts for Dormobile campers
www.dormobile.uk.com
01794 830831

FBIVW – sales, Splitty and Bay, plus parts
www.fbivw.com
01792 585544

VW Heritage
– parts and accessories
www.vwheritage.com
0845 873 8328

Interior Motive – camper interiors
www.interiormotiveuk.com
07830 183190

Just Kampers
– parts, accessories & chat forums
www.justkampers.com
0845 1204720

Karmann Konnection – restoration parts,
accessories and vehicle sales
www.karmannkonnection.com
01702 601155

Mega-Bug – parts
www.megabug.co.uk
020 8317 7333

Alan H. Schofield Classic Volkswagen
Restoration Parts
www.ahschofield.co.uk
01457 854 267

L. R. Superbeetles – Sales, repairs,
restorations and spares
www.superbeetles.co.uk
01206 563433

Status VW – parts for air-cooled VWs
www.status-vw.co.uk
0870 143 1445

VW Curtains
– curtains and interiors for campers
www.vwcurtains.com
0701 7436601

VW Downunder – sales and camper hire
www.vwdownunder.com
01375 675550

Wolfsburg VW's Type 2 Specialists
– vehicle sales and restorations
www.wolfsburgvw.com
01254 830432

## REGULAR SHOWS FOR TRANSPORTER ENTHUSIASTS

April
Bus Types – Oswestry, Shropshire
www.bus-types.co.uk

May
Stanford Hall – Nr Lutterworth,
Leicestershire
www.stanfordhallvw.co.uk

Vanwest – Haynes International Motor
Museum, Sparkford, Somerset
www.vanwest.net

June
Bristol Volksfest
www.bristolvolksfest.co.uk

The Bus Stopover – Wymeswold,
Leicestershire
www.thebusstopover.com

September
Vanfest – Three Counties Showground,
Malvern, Worcestershire
www.vanfest.org

September/October
Brighton Breeze
www.ssvc.org.uk

# INDEX